Russia's Lost Literature of the Absurd
_____*A Literary Discovery*

Russia's Lost Literature of the Absurd
————————————*A Literary Discovery*

SELECTED WORKS OF
Daniil Kharms and Alexander Vvedensky

EDITED AND
TRANSLATED BY *George Gibian*

Cornell University Press | ITHACA AND LONDON

First published 1971 by Cornell University Press.
Published in the United Kingdom by Cornell University
Press Ltd., 2–4 Brook Street, London W1Y 1AA.

International Standard Book Number 0-8014-0653-6
Library of Congress Catalog Card Number 74-160847

PRINTED IN THE UNITED STATES OF AMERICA
BY VAIL-BALLOU PRESS, INC.

Contents

95617

Preface

Texts of these works came into my possession in Eastern Europe during the last few years. Incredible as it may seem, these amazing pieces, written in Soviet Russia forty years ago, belong with Western absurdist literature of the present day. The authors were members of the literary and artistic circle which called itself Oberiu (a name formed from the initials of the Russian words for Association for Real Art). The group was active in Leningrad between 1927 and 1930, and some of its members continued to write, with no hope of publication, through the 1930's. They came under attack and were silenced. Daniil Kharms and Alexander Vvedensky were arrested shortly after the outbreak of World War II, and perished early in 1942.

Their works continued to circulate, as happens frequently in Russia, in manuscripts, privately typed and passed around among friends. With the exception of a very few stories, these writings have never been published in the Soviet Union. A small volume of Kharms's works in German translation was published in 1970. One of the plays is included in the German volume and has also been printed in a Polish translation. A few of Kharms's shorter pieces have appeared in English translation in a review in *Atlas* magazine.

When I was in Soviet Russia and elsewhere in Eastern Europe in 1965–1966 and in 1968, doing research on the avant-garde in Russian culture after 1917, I began to hear about this strange group. I managed to find typewritten manuscripts of a few of their works and came to regard them as an important, hitherto missing link in the chain of absurd and black-humor writings, which we in the West think of as stretching from Jarry, Tzara, and Kafka through the Surrealists to Ionesco, Albee, and Beckett. The Oberiu works are grotesque, funny, wild, and disturbing. I made an effort to find out all I could about these writers—whom Soviet Russian officialdom and police made into unpersons—and to assemble all I could of their writings.

Viewing these impressive remains, the literary historian is dismayed to discover that the authors were almost completely wiped out of memory and history by the Soviet state. Yet the group was an important part of the modernist movement of the 1920's in Russia. Few Westerners know of Kharms and Vvedensky, yet these two writers have a place in literary history and deserve to be widely known for their accomplishments.

Plans are now under way to publish as complete an edition as is possible of the Oberiu works in the original Russian. It is gratifying to me to be able to present a selection in English translation.

Works that have circulated only in manuscript present great textual problems. I have seen only one version of most of the pieces. Obvious typing and other errors are remarkably few. I tried to translate closely, without editorial omissions and other changes. If, as I very much hope, the day comes when more works by Kharms and Vvedensky are published inside the Soviet Union or reach us abroad, variants of texts translated in this book may crop up. It may then be possible to publish a larger collection in English and to base it upon several different texts. The works in the present volume are a selection of the best texts available at this time.

My work on the Oberiuty (members of the Oberiu) was generously supported by the Committee on Soviet Studies of Cornell University, to which I am grateful; I owe thanks also to the American Council of Learned Societies, which made possible my stay in the Soviet Union in 1965–1966. The Russian Institute of Columbia University, by appointing me a Research Associate for 1969–1970, gave me time for research and access to libraries in New York City. I used part of that period for work on these translations, as well as on the Russian edition. I am grateful to the Director of the Russian Institute, Professor Marshall Shulman, and others on the staff of Columbia University.

Professor John Malmstad of Columbia University and Professor Robin Milner-Gulland of the University of Sussex were exceptionally helpful. Professor Antonia Glasse, my colleague in the Department of Russian Literature at Cornell, improved my translations and suggested ingenious ways to cope with Kharms's and Vvedensky's often very difficult idiom. I should like to thank the staff of Olin Library, at Cornell University, for helping me, as always, in every way imaginable.

In the last stages of the preparation of this book, I had the good fortune to locate Kharms's widow, who is now living in South America and had the kindness to send me valuable information about him, for which I am very grateful.

GEORGE GIBIAN

King Ferry, New York

INTRODUCTION: Daniil Kharms and Alexander Vvedensky

BY GEORGE GIBIAN

The members of the Oberiu, the literary group to which
Daniil Kharms and Alexander Vvedensky belonged, called
themselves "natural thinkers." They combated the petrification,
immobility of taste, and hypocrisy of the world around them.
They saw the ironies in their surroundings and displayed
irony in their writings. Vvedensky once said, "The feeling for
the illogicality of the world and its fragmentation has the
upper hand in me." Kharms's sensitivity toward suffering
intensified his reactions. In 1939 he wrote, "Once I saw a fight
between a fly and a bug. It was so terrible I ran out into the
street and ran God knows where."

The political climate in Russia between 1927 and 1935 was
antipathetic to everything Kharms, Vvedensky, and their
colleagues were trying to do. Literature of "social command"
and, later, of "socialistic realism" was being demanded. In
1930, the black-humor writers Kharms and Vvedensky were
attacked bitterly in the press. Soon afterward all that was left
for them was to publish children's stories. Both writers were
arrested in 1941. Kharms was jailed on August 23, 1941. On
February 4, 1942, when his wife came to leave a parcel for
him at the prison hospital, she was told that he had died on
February 2. There are conflicting versions of Vvedensky's
death; but we do know it occurred somewhere in the

Ukraine, also in the early stages of the war. Their gruesome deaths are like occurrences in their own works.

The typewritten texts of two of their plays, which had been produced but never published in Russia, and of numerous prose works and poems (also mostly unpublished) continued to circulate among small groups of readers in Leningrad. In the 1960's, Polish and Czech theater people and journalists found out about Kharms's and Vvedensky's works, tracked down some of their writings in Russia, and translated and published a few of them. Kharms's "Elizaveta Bam" was performed in Warsaw and published in *Dialog*, a Polish magazine specializing in avant-garde literature. Two Czech magazines also published extracts from the prose and verse of these writers.

Guarded references to the Oberiu group and to its members, who called themselves Oberiuty, began to appear in print in Soviet Russia: a line or two here and there in an article, paragraphs in books about children's literature; finally brief essays about them were published. The best accounts—though very short—were those in an obscure learned publication, almost unavailable in the West—a report of papers read at a student conference about literature held at the University of Tartu, in Soviet Estonia, in 1967.[1]

---

[1] The account of Kharms's and Vvedensky's lives and literary careers in this introduction is greatly indebted to two articles in a collection of student papers, both written jointly by Anatoly Alexandrov and Mikhail Meilakh: "Tvorchestvo Daniila Kharmsa" and "Tvorchestvo A. Vvedenskogo," in *Materialy XXII Nauchnoy Studencheskoy konferentsii, Tartuskii Gosudarstvenny Universitet* (Tartu, 1967), pp. 101–104 and 105–109. Anatoly Alexandrov has also supplied much additional information about the Oberiuty in two articles published in

I tried to learn as much as I could about Daniil Kharms, Alexander Vvedensky and their colleagues, and finally, in 1969 and 1970, I succeeded in assembling the texts of the chief works. The present volume presents translations of selections.

II

Daniil Ivanovich Kharms was born in Petersburg in 1905. His real name was Yuvachev, but he liked to use various pseudonyms; Kharms was the one under which he wrote most often. His father, an intellectual and a revolutionary under the tsars, belonged to the People's Freedom (Narodnaya Volya) group and was arrested and sentenced to life imprisonment. He was imprisoned in the Peter and Paul Fortress, then in Schlüsselburg, and finally sent to exile on the island of Sakhalin; he was freed in 1900. Like his son later, he wrote fiction—stories of fantasy. He sent several to Leo Tolstoy. In a letter dated March 1, 1906, Tolstoy's wife wrote to Kharms's father, "Last night we read aloud 'The Schlüsselburg Fort' and 'Monastery Prisons' "; and on April 6, 1909, "Tonight we read 'Celestial Court.' When I asked Leo Tolstoy what I should write to you, he said it was well written but that he personally does not in general like anything fantastic but loves clarity and simplicity in everything. Of course he has nothing against your works being printed. Personally I like that story; it is written with inspiration and

Czechoslovakia: "Oberiu: Predvaritel'nye zametki," *Československá rusistika*, XIII, No. 5 (1968), 296–303; and "Ignavia" (an essay in Czech accompanied by Czech translations by Václav Daněk of Oberiu works), *Světová literatura*, No. 6 (1968), pp. 156–174.

lightly, not heavily, and in spite of its fantastic quality, one does not feel anything false in it." [2]

Kharms's father used to invite him to his study, set him on his knee, and tell or read him his "fantastic stories." The taste for fantasy was even stronger in the son. Kharms not only wrote verse, drama, and fantastic stories, but he also made his life into a work of absurd fantasy. His pranks and eccentricities somewhat resembled those of his Western European counterparts, Alfred Jarry, Francis Picabia, Guillaume Apollinaire, and Tristan Tzara, but in the supposedly classless and revolutionary Soviet society in which he lived his behavior was not merely incongruous; it was also provocative. Trainloads of people accused of being former noblemen were being deported from Leningrad at the time Kharms affected aristocratic mannerisms in a desperate game of insubordination.

Among his pranks was the invention of a brother who, he asserted, was a Privatdozent at the University of Petersburg, and whose mannerisms (and mustache) he pretended to copy. When he went to a tavern, he made a point of bringing silver cups, family heirlooms; he would take them out of a briefcase and drink only from them. When he went to the theater, he pasted on a false mustache, saying that it was indecent for a man to go to the theater without one.

Vvedensky said about him, "Kharms is art." He was not the only agent in turning his life into a work of black humor and absurdity; the Soviet state collaborated. Kharms's writings

---

[2] The letters are quoted by N. Khalatov in his postscripts about Kharms at the end of the volume of Kharms's children's works which Khalatov edited, *Chto eto bylo?* (Moscow, 1967).

reflect the phantasmagoria of a country where, since 1914, the bottom dropped out of things repeatedly, where events conditioned people to believe that nothing could be trusted, that the stuff of nightmares could be encountered in everyday life.

One of Kharms's friends, Vladimir Lifshits, wrote in his recollections of the poet that his room was sparsely, ascetically furnished. In one corner a strange object stood out in the almost empty room. It was made of pieces of iron, wooden boards, empty cigarette boxes, springs, bicycle wheels, twine, and cans. When Lifshits asked what it was, Kharms replied, "A machine." "What kind of machine?" "No kind. Just a machine in general." "And where does it come from?" "I put it together myself," Kharms said proudly. "What does it do?" "It does nothing." "What do you mean nothing?" "Simply nothing." "What is it for?" "I just wanted to have a machine at home." He did not call it a collage, a sculpture, or an *objet trouvé*—it was simply a machine to do nothing.[3]

Just as in his writings he created humorous fantasy, so out of his life he wrought a work of taboo-shattering, dangerous, funny art. His writings and his life were exploits of courage, propelling him toward saintly and comic martyrdom.

Over his piano Kharms had placed a piece of paper with the inscription: "Here are read Gogol, Hamsun, Glinka, and especially Bach." His favorite literary hero was Nagel in Knut Hamsun's *Mystery* (who spoke the words, "I am a stranger among my own people. Soon my hour will come"). His drawers were full of manuscripts, including drafts of farces, and

---

[3] Vladimir Lifshits, "Mozhet byt', prigoditsya," *Voprosy literatury*, No. 1 (1969), pp. 242–243.

phonograph records. Kharms loved acting and the stage. He often said, "Art is a cupboard." He recited his poems at Oberiu literary evenings, hopping around the stage among canvas representations of cupboards.

In order to round up an audience for a literary evening of the Oberiu group, Kharms once crawled out on the cornice of the fifth floor of the House of the Book in Leningrad (a building which housed various editorial offices, including that of the children's magazines for which he worked) and walked around on it, his back to the wall of the building, smoking a pipe, wearing spats, plus fours, and a checked jacket. From time to time he would take the pipe out of his mouth and shout down to the crowd on the sidewalk below, "Everybody come to the literary evening of the Oberiuty!" The crowd gaped as he walked along the ledge, but a huge audience did come.

Like many clowns, comedians, and writers of comedy, Kharms suffered from melancholia. He even gave his own personal blues a feminine proper name: Ignavia. In order to combat Ignavia, he wrote a poem that served him as a charm or incantation against her. When Ignavia approached, he would recite this poem in an effort to ward her off:

> I looked for a long time at the green trees.
> Peace filled my mind.
> As before, I still don't have any great, extraordinary ideas.
> The same scraps, fragments, and tail ends.
> Either earthy desires flame up
> Or I reach for an interesting book
> Or suddenly a sweet dream knocks on my head.
> I sit down by the window in a deep armchair.

I look at the clock, light a pipe,
But suddenly I jump up and walk over to the table,
Sit down in a hard chair and roll myself a cigarette.
I see a little spider running on the wall.
I watch him, can't tear myself away.
He is stopping me from picking up my pen.
I must kill that spider!
But I'm too lazy to get up.
Now I look inside myself,
But inside me it is empty, monotonous, and boring.
Intense life beats nowhere.
Everything is limp and sleepy, like wet straw.
So I have traveled inside myself
And now I'm standing here before you.
You are waiting to hear what I'll tell you about my journey.
But I'm silent because I saw nothing there.
Leave me alone to look quietly at the green trees.
Then maybe peace will fill my mind.
Then maybe my mind will wake up,
And I will wake up, and my intense life will start beating
      inside me.

Kharms's literary debut took place in 1925, when he was
twenty. He participated in a public reading of poetry in
Leningrad—the locale of all the later Oberiu activity. In the
next year, 1926, came his first publication, one of the very few
he was ever to see, except for his children's stories. An
anthology of verse by the Union of Leningrad Poets included
his "Incident on the Railway," a poem with disjointed phrases,
deliberate incoherence, and a very marked rhythm, rather like
a meter of Finnish folklore poetry, familiar to us through
Longfellows's *Hiawatha*. The strands of images and the

trochaic beat strengthen the feeling of joyous holiday travel, play, and the outdoors.

III

Alexander Vvedensky, who was born in 1904 in Petersburg, studied briefly at the University of Petersburg in 1921 and gave his first public poetry reading in 1926. While he was still in secondary school (gymnasium), he sent his poems to the poets Alexander Blok and Nikolai Gumilyov. A few of his poems were published in 1926 in an anthology, and again in 1927 in the volume *Kostyor* ("Bonfire"). Except for numerous children's stories later, no other works by Vvedensky were published in Russia during his lifetime.

All the literary activity of Kharms and Vvedensky, with the exception of the publication of a handful of poems, took place outside the world of print. It consisted of readings, literary evenings, the circulation of manuscripts among friends, performances of plays, and programs of mixed skits, dramatic scenes, poetry readings, and lectures. Its manifestations were not sharply defined or fixed in the set form of the book or magazine, but ephemeral, changeable, multiform—in poems recited but not recorded, or recorded in the informal medium of handwritten or typewritten pages.

By the spring of 1926, a fairly well-defined group consisting of five poets and one prose writer had been formed. Nikolai Oleinikov was a poet and the author of many satirical humorous works; he was editor of the children's magazine *Chizh*. Doyvber Levin, about whom little is known, wrote prose. Igor Bakhterev was a stage and film director. Nikolai Zabolotsky later became by far the most widely known author of the group. His early verse was Futuristic and rather mannered. His connection with the Oberiuty is sometimes hinted at in introductions to Soviet editions and discussions of his works or mentioned apologetically. In the 1930's, Zabolotsky abandoned his youthful experimentation, and was widely published. His participation in the Oberiu group in the 1920's, as well as the collaboration with the Oberiuty by such major painters as Pavel Nikolaevich Filonov and Kasimir Malevich, suggests that if social and political pressures in Soviet Russia after 1928 had not warped the development of Russian culture, an absurdist–black-humor movement like that of Kharms and Vvedensky might have become a major and dominant current.

In 1926, Kharms was already dreaming of an Oberiu theater, to be called Radix. Various semitheatrical performances were presented. In the fall of 1926, the group began rehearsing for a dramatic show which was to have the absurd title "My Mother All in Watches." It was to be a mosaic of poems by Vvedensky and Kharms, linked into a continuous spectacle. However, a public performance did not materialize for "technical reasons."

An evening was described in this entry in Kharms's notebook:

This Friday [November 12, 1926] I want to arrange situations of conflict which will include these: After our reading, Igor Bakhterev will come on and give a nonsense speech with quotations from unknown poets. Then [name illegible] will come out and also give a speech, but with a Marxist slant. In this speech, he will defend us. At the end, two unknown people will come up to the lectern hand in hand and declare: "We cannot say very much about what has been read, but we shall sing something." And they will sing something.

Gaga Katzman will come on last. He will relate something out of the lives of Saints. That will be good.[4]

Kharms collaborated with a number of writers as well as with leading artists. He associated with Kasimir Malevich, the painter whose "White on White" had been one of the earliest and most extreme landmarks of world abstractionism, and who in his Suprematist treatises and essays formulated an ideology for the modernist turning away from representation of the natural world to the creation of new pure forms and balanced designs. Malevich was the friend and mentor of many poets and artists in Leningrad. He headed the Institute of Artistic Culture (Inkhuk, dissolved in 1928), where many meetings as well as rehearsals, performances, and poetry readings of the Oberiu took place. The close association of people working in various genres of art and literature was one of the outstanding features of avant-garde cultural life in Russia before and after the Revolution. The Oberiu in this regard resembled the earlier Futurists and other Russian modernists.

Another painter close to the Oberiuty was Pavel Nikolaevich Filonov, almost unknown in the West but very influential in Russia. Filonov is still not exhibited in Russian museums, but hundreds of his canvases have been preserved in Russia, and his theory and practice have been of primary importance and continue to influence the youngest generation of Russian

---

[4] Quoted in Alexandrov, "Oberiu," p. 297. The Oberiut Igor Bakhterev became best known as the coauthor of the play "Commander Suvorov," which he wrote jointly with Alexander Razumovsky of the film section of the Oberiu. See I. Rakhtanov, " 'Yozh' i 'Chizh,' " in *Detskaya literatura* ("Children's Literature"), No. 2 (Moscow, 1962), p. 137.

painters today.[5] The theater director Igor Terentev, famous for a bold avant-garde production of Gogol's *Inspector General*, in 1927, was also in the group.[6]

In 1928 the Oberiuty were ready with a manifesto which was formulated by Kharms, the poet Zabolotsky, and others. It was printed in the irregularly appearing periodical *Afishi doma pechati* ("Posters of the House of the Press"), No. 2 (1928), and was frequently recited from the stage. The views it set forth must be judged against the background of the cultural situation in Russia in 1928.

Before World War I, several of Russia's poets and painters had been in the vanguard of world modernism. Some of their work done in the first two decades of this century anticipated trends that have been evident throughout the world since then. Vasily Kandinsky, Naum Gabo, Marc Chagall, and Vladimir Mayakovsky are internationally known; others (such as Pavel Filonov) undeservedly remained unknown abroad and even at home.

---

[5] The only extended discussion of this important and neglected painter is the Czech book by Jan Kříž, *Pavel Nikolajevič Filonov* (Prague, 1966).

[6] Igor Gerasimovich Terentev was the author of numerous Futurist works. He belonged also to the group of poets who called themselves Forty-one Degrees and to LEF (Left Front of Art). See Vladimir Markov, *Russian Futurism: A History* (Berkeley and Los Angeles, 1968), pp. 358–362. In 1924 Igor Terentev had directed a play called *John Reed*, based on the American journalist's involvement in the Bolshevik Revolution, in an extremely antirealistic, antiacademic production. His iconoclastic *Inspector General* was even more famous. Terentev published his views of the theater in the journal *Novy LEF* ("New LEF"). An account of Terentev's work in the theater is given by S. L. Tsimbal in *Raznye teatral'nye vremena* ("Various Ages in the Theater") (Leningrad, 1969), pp. 279–281 and 393–396.

Even before the Revolution, Malevich in painting and Velemir Khlebnikov in poetry (to name only two outstanding leaders) had proclaimed their rejection of old "laws" and their search for new ones—in their own lives, in society, and in art. The war, the Revolution, and the Civil War pushed the process still further. As Mayakovsky once wrote, the violence of World War I made a Futurist of everyone. Everything that had to do with stability and norms of expectancy, with what may be taken for granted, was destroyed. Kharms and Vvedensky belonged to the last wave of postrevolutionary writers who were able to express the new sense of uncertainty and rejection and of eagerness for novelty.

The literary scene in Russia after 1917 was made up of many schools and splinter groups, which in turn kept subdividing and disappearing. However, classification, albeit oversimplified, is possible according to two criteria based on sets of antithetical attitudes. The first is whether the basic outlook of a group favored Marxism, or "social command"—in other words, art (painting, drama, or poetry) that threw in its lot with didactic, pro-Soviet, socially conscious aims—or repudiated such social aims altogether, or at least subordinated them and emphasized artistic goals. The second is whether a group preferred realistic, conventional, traditional artistic methods (nineteenth-century realism in literature, academic representation of nature in painting) or radical experimentation (revolutionary innovations in literature, abstraction in painting). The traditional in art usually went hand in hand with lucidity, clarity, ease of understanding, and accessibility to broad groups of uneducated readers, the experimental, with orientation toward coteries, cliques, sophisticated small groups of potential readers, and obscurity due to complex, difficult artistic techniques.

In the 1920's various schools, groups, and styles coexisted. They fought among themselves and argued back and forth, but no one group had a monopoly of power. The pro-Revolutionary, socially conscious writers were not always the most conservative in artistic technique. On the contrary, some leading pro-Marxist, pro-Soviet writers—the outstanding example is Mayakovsky—also were most fervid in the desire for artistic innovation. Many confused being "revolutionary" in artistic methods with being revolutionary in politics.

Various "Proletarian Art" groups, however, attacked the "left" schools. The Proletarian factions demanded a message, lucid style, and that writers keep in mind the audience of uneducated workers and write for and to them. In 1928 RAPP (the Association of Proletarian Writers) was given power over literary life in Soviet Russia (it was replaced in 1932 by the Union of Writers).

The Oberiu was an anachronism in the Soviet Union of the First Five-Year Plan. Its ideas and practice followed in a straight line from the most extreme modernism of the period immediately after 1917, whereas from 1928 on, Russia was a more and more tightly controlled society, with RAPP ideas, and later, socialistic realism enforced in literature as well as in the other arts. (The key years of Oberiu activity, 1928–1930, overlapped with the last three years of Mayakovsky's life, during which he was being hounded by the Proletarians.)

"The Oberiu Manifesto," in some of its sections, carried on a polemic with the Proletarian groups—a polemic not likely to get the Oberiuty very far, since the press and all the instruments of power were against them. The Oberiu anti-Proletarian attack was two-pronged. On the one hand the "Manifesto" tried to occupy ground claimed by the Proletarians. The Oberiuty affirmed that they, not the Proletarian writers, truly filled the need of the new society and supplied, or would supply, art worthy of the new classless Soviet people. The Proletarian writers, they asserted, were not doing the job: their books were piling up in warehouses; the Soviet people would not read them.

The Oberiu went on to assert that "artistic methods of the old schools" could not satisfy the proletariat. Proletarian art was old-fashioned and a failure; the Oberiuty, on the other hand, "penetrate into the center" and "seek an organically new concept of life and a new approach to things."

The Oberiu, however, also defined itself carefully in relation to various non-Proletarian groups. It was easy for the Oberiuty to differentiate themselves from the Proletarians: that was a matter of two opposites. It is more difficult to separate the Oberiu from various kindred Futurist groups. A primary distinction is that the Oberiu rejected pure formalism, or art for art's sake. "The Oberiu Manifesto" did not oppose the view that art ought to concern itself with life and reality. It claimed that Oberiu art was realistic, that it did concern itself with life: "It finds a way to represent any subject." The "Manifesto" did not view art as separate from life or as an autonomous realm. Art was to be related to life; it ought to be a representation of life, but not a complete or slavish imitation or reproduction.

The second great watershed in the "Manifesto" was the disjunction between the Oberiu and *zaum*. Before and after

1917, some of the more extreme Futurists wrote what they called *zaum* verse—transsense, or transreason (*um* means "reason" or "intelligence"; *za* signifies the prefix "trans"). One scholar has distinguished five different kinds of *zaum* poetry in the work of one poet, Velemir Khlebnikov. A common denominator of *zaum* writing is its move away from the referential meaning of language. It perhaps comes as close as art in the medium of words can come to abstraction in painting. Sometimes poetry is composed of made-up sounds (not Russian words but new combinations of sounds), either entirely or mixed to some extent with existing words. Some *zaum* consists of neologisms, new formations, and some (which comes very close to surrealism) of "real" words, words that exist in Russian, but so joined together that they are not intelligible to discursive reason.

"The Oberiu Manifesto" rejects *zaum* in unequivocal terms: "We are enemies of those who castrate the word and turn it into an impotent and useless mongrel." However, while the Oberiuty assert their intention to "broaden the meaning of the object and of the word," they do intend "to peel away its literary and everyday skin"; "the collisions of verbal meanings" are to give birth to a new object, different from that we see in life. They want to clear away what they consider outmoded literary conventions and to present us with a new object— shocking, distorted, changed, but still real. The word *predmet* ("object") occurs often; there is strong emphasis in Oberiu theory on objectivity, "thingness."

The "Manifesto" stresses the individual, component parts of a literary work. The separate parts of a work of art are to be given autonomy—independence from conventional plots, structures, connections. (The concept of free development of individual component parts bears a striking resemblance to the theories of the American-Armenian painter Arshile Gorky.)

The sections of the "Manifesto" dealing with the film and with theater are very important. They develop further the implications of the Oberiu attitudes toward *zaum* and the word. The Oberiu desires not only to emphasize the component elements of art and communication (in poetry, the word; in the film and theater, the individual scene or fragment of action), but to juxtapose them with others, linking or connecting them in startling ways. The individual parts are not to be distorted or to be changed beyond recognition. The phrase, the gesture, the conversation are "realistic." The shock comes through the novel combinations of these units. The plays "Elizabeth Bam" and "Christmas at the Ivanovs' " demonstrate the creation of shock. They swing joltingly from eulogy, from the high and exalted, to parody and low life, from solemnity to sordidness. The Oberiuty—like various Futurist groups before them—spoke often of *sdvig* (a sudden wrenching, a jolt, a shift—from the word for "geological fault"). One most frequently notices *sdvig* in their works at the points of juncture, where abrupt, jarring jumps take place from one type of discourse to another, from one stylistic level to another. During most of the nineteenth century literary conventions had largely idealized unity and coherence. The Oberiu rejected these conventions and enshrined their opposites.

Kharms was close to the "Left Wing" of a group which called itself the Union of Poets, particularly A. Tufanov. Tufanov's last book, *Ushkuyniki,* was published in 1927. It tried to combine the ideas of Einstein and Bergson with *zaum* literary techniques.[7] Tufanov's poems drew on Old Russian literature and history, on folklore, and on Novgorodian folk and dialectal expressions. Kharms likewise turned to folk dialect, to Soviet everyday prosaisms, and to the folk drama of the fair (puppet plays and peepshows). He also dipped into the lore and techniques of children's literature: violence, avoidance of psychologizing and explaining, abrupt switches, naïveté, speed.

In 1927, Kharms put together a manuscript collection of his poems, which he entitled "The Administration of Things: Difficult-to-Understand Verses." His introduction read:

To the Reader:
Reader, I am afraid you will not understand my verses. You would understand them if you became acquainted with them gradually, perhaps in various magazines. But you did not have that opportunity. With an aching heart I publish my first book of poems.

To the Reviewer:
First of all, before saying anything about the formal defects of my poems, read "The Administration of Things" from cover to cover. Secondly, before you put me down as one of the Futurists of the past decade, read them and then read me a second time.[8]

---

[7] Tufanov was the author also of the important article "Metrika, ritmika i instrumentallizatsia narodnykh chastushek" ("Metrics, Rhythmics, and Orchestration in Folk *Chastushi*") *Izvestiia Arkhangelskogo obshchestva izucheniia russkago severa* ("Publications of the Archangel Society for the Study of the Russian North"), January– February 1919, pp. 13–23. See discussions of Tufanov in Markov, *Russian Futurism*, p. 348, and in Alexandrov's article "Oberiu." Markov's book is the best general work about Russian Futurism.

[8] Quoted in Alexandrov, "Oberiu," p. 298.

The Oberiuty, in 1927, made frequent appearances (in readings and spectacles) at the Union of Poets, in the Institute for Art History, in student dormitories, and even in military barracks. There were plans for the publication of an "Almanac," an anthology of the Radix group, which was to include works by the artists Malevich, Filonov, and Dmitriev, the critics Viktor Shklovsky and Tsimbal, and the poets Zabolotsky, Kharms, Vvedensky, Tufanov, and Vaginov. However, the publication of the "Manifesto" in January 1928 and the successful performance of Kharms's "Elizabeth Bam" (during the Oberiu theatrical evening "Three Left Hours") in the Leningrad House of the Press called attention to the group, with disastrous consequences. The officials overseeing organized literary evenings became frightened. *Krasnaya Gazeta* ("Red Newspaper") called the Oberiu evening "extreme *zaum*," "nonsense," and "frankly cynical confusion." Thereafter the Oberiu was able to appear only on small stages and in obscure meeting places.

Toward the end of 1928 the Oberiu planned a typical evening performance. With its mixture of genres, it sounded more like a circus or a variety show than a legitimate stage play. The program was to include the following:

Lecture by Dr. Tinvey.
Doyvber Levin—eucalic prose.
Daniil Kharms—objects and figures.
Aleksey Pastukhov—the same (Pastukhov was a magician—A. A.)
Igor Bakhterev—forks and verses.
Alexander Vvedensky—self-observation over a wall.
Bovaldis—three (acrobats—A. A.)
The Central Cupboard (a choral reading—A. A.)

Theatrical act "Winter Walk." Tragedy with music, by I. V.
Bakhterev and D. I. Kharms. Music by P. A. Volfius. With
A. Y. Grin, E. I. Vigiliansky, Fedya Tykin.

. . . . .

Vasili Oberiutov
Directed by Evg. Vigiliansky.[9]

Clearly, a jocular air dominates the program; there are
numerous untranslatable comic items, as well as puns and
nonsensical skits. The fictitious signature "Oberiutov" recalls
one literary ancestor of the group: Kozma Prutkov, the
collective *nom de plume* under which two Zhemchuzhnikov
brothers and A. K. Tolstoy composed a series of comic plays
and poems in the nineteenth century. The performance did not
take place, but the playlet "Winter Walk" was performed in
1929, in the House of the Press.

The last theatrical spectacle of the Oberiu was presented in
the Leningrad University student dormitory in April 1930.
Kharms, Levin, and Vladimirov took part. A few days later
(April 9, 1930) the Leningrad newspaper *Smena* attacked the
program in an article entitled "Reactionary Jugglerism:
About One Sortie of Literary Hooligans," which charged that
"nonsense poetry" was "a protest against the dictatorship of
the proletariat."

Performances stopped; the group ceased to exist even as a
semiorganized entity. Kharms, Vvedensky, and Zabolotsky
continued to see one another informally, most often in the
apartment of the poet and children's writer L. Savel'ev, and

---

[9] *Ibid.*, p. 303. Kharms's term *evkalicheskaya* ("eucalic") is a
neologism. Alexandrov added and initialed the explanations in
parentheses.

planned to collaborate on a book, "Archimedes' Tub." Like many of their plans and projects, this one was never realized.

Kharms and Vvedensky began to write more and more for children. They were close friends of the famous editor and author of fables and children's poetry, Samuil Marshak, and collaborated with him in two magazines specifically for children, *Chizh* and *Yozh*. Vvedensky, in addition to verses and stories in the magazines, published about sixty children's books between 1928 and 1940; Kharms wrote many children's stories and a smaller number of books.[10]

Most of these stories and verses for children were just a means of making a living and of holding some kind of official position, or job, at a time when repression made other literary work impossible for Kharms and Vvedensky. Some of the writing is crude hack work, the kind of propaganda then in demand. One story, for instance, was published by Vvedensky in the magazine *Chizh* in 1931. Ironically, it deals with Christmas trees, a subject he was then also treating, in a very different manner, in the play "Christmas at the Ivanovs'."

Vvedensky gave the magazine just what was wanted. In his story children were asked by their teacher whether any of them would have a Christmas tree at home and would go to

---

[10] Evgeny Shvarts and Nikolai Oleinikov, then editors in the Children's Section of the State Publishing House, after an Oberiu evening in the early spring of 1927, issued the first invitation to Kharms, Vvedensky, and their colleagues to write for children. Details about this meeting and much other valuable information can be found in I. Bakhterev and A. Razumovsky, "O Nikolae Oleinikove," in *Den' poezii* ("The Day of Poetry") (Moscow, 1964), pp. 154–160. Rakhtanov's article " 'Yozh' i 'Chizh' " contains a wealth of information about Kharms, Vvedensky, and children's magazines of the period.

church. (This was a period when the Communists were struggling to eliminate survivals of Christmas customs.) Only one child, Shura, raised her hand. She explained that her mother justified having a tree by claiming that if they did not have one, the girl would cry. The other children and the teacher explained to the girl that one did not need to have a tree, invited her mother to school, and explained this to her, convincing her not to have a tree. Then, in school, instead of having a Christmas celebration and a tree, all the children met and happily sang antireligious songs. Neither the girl nor anybody else cried; everybody saw that it was much better not to have a tree.

Several of the children's stories by the Oberiuty, however, reveal the same imaginativeness and some of the same devices that are found in Kharms's and Vvedensky's absurd and black-humor stories, verse, and drama for adults, which abound in quick action, repetition, and shifts from one plane to another. In fact, such devices are more characteristic of stories for children than of literature for adults. The turn to writing for children, besides being a concession to the times and a yielding to necessity, was also a very natural, logical move for Kharms and Vvedensky. Children's thinking is not tightly restricted by habitual logical schemes, it is freely associative, and it is concrete—all characteristics which fascinated Kharms and Vvedensky.

Kharms's and Vvedensky's children's stories often have the structure of a series of incidents which is repetitious without increment in meaning. The world in which the characters live is often hazy and mysterious; the environment and the characters are out of step with one another. Events are difficult to understand. There are misunderstandings about language. Malapropisms are used; words and names which sound alike are confused.

Even in his work for children, Kharms kept in touch with Russia's leading artists. One of his books, *Vo pervykh i vo vtorykh* ("First and Secondly"), was illustrated by Vladimir Tatlin, one of the most imaginative innovators in Soviet design and architecture of the post-1917 era.

Like Kharms's works for adults, his children's stories upset conventions. Unusual connections are made. In one story, for example, porcupines cry, "Cock-a-doodle-doo." Sometimes Kharms assumes that a real, substantive relationship exists between an animal and its name, as when he says that only a very clever man can guess which of seven cats pictured in a story has which of seven names.

However, unlike the stories for grownups, the children's tales are usually comforting, at least in the end. They are not nightmares but dreams of wish fulfillment. Children who very much want an airplane ride get one; they go to Brazil, or at least they think they do; then they arrive home again, and are even given a ride in a car as a bonus.

One typical children's story by Kharms, published in 1929, ties in closely with his tendency in works for adults to create characters who are alienated, misplaced. In "How an Old Woman Went Shopping for Ink," an old woman goes to buy some ink. She tries a butcher shop, a fish store, and finally the editorial offices of a children's magazine, each time without realizing she is in the wrong place. She is hard of hearing, which leads to various misunderstandings. Like Nagel in Knut Hamsun's *Mystery*, who we saw was Kharms's favorite literary

hero, she is an outsider. In the summer she asks where the
snow is; in a kerosene store she asks for French rolls. Her
husband has died; her son has grown up and left her. She
lives alone and drinks tea, quite out of touch with contemporary
Soviet life; she naïvely and ignorantly stumbles around. The
editors of the children's magazine finally write about her in a
story for children.

In 1937, Kharms published a little children's song which
was sadly prophetic of events to come. The main point of it
was that "a man walked out of his house," and "from that time
on, from that time on, he was gone." It concluded with the
lines:

> But if somehow it should happen
> That you meet him somewhere
>   Very quickly
>   Very quickly
> Very quickly come and tell us.

A short time later Daniil Kharms himself walked out of his
house, disappeared, and was gone forever. In 1956, Kharms's
relatives were informed that he had been "posthumously
rehabilitated."

In the 1950's and 1960's the name of the Oberiu group
cropped up here and there in Soviet books about children's
literature, and brief references to members of the circle
appeared in various memoirs.[11] Discussions of the history of

---

[11] In Soviet Russia, Kharms and Vvedensky are officially regarded
solely as children's authors. The bibliography of children's literature,
Sovietskie detskie pisateli: Bibliograficheskii slovar (Moscow, 1961),
lists the basic dates of Kharms's life and his chief children's works on
p. 385, and Vvedensky's on p. 73.

Soviet Russian literature for children have occasionally referred to Kharms as a fine model too rarely imitated, outstanding in his lightness of touch and power of imagination. The references have a mysterious flavor which hints that their subject must be treated somewhat delicately—that more is implied than it would have been wise to blurt out in full. In 1967 and 1968, a few snippets from Kharms's writings were published in *Literaturnaya gazeta* ("Literary Newspaper") and elsewhere. Brief articles about him appeared in several Soviet magazines (one, in the popular monthly *Yunost'* ["Youth"] by the poet Boris Slutsky), and a volume of selections from Kharms's children's stories and poems was published in 1967, with an appreciative postscript. The two young scholars who read papers about Kharms and Vvedensky at a student conference on literature which was held in Tartu (Estonia) in 1967 have assembled, or at least located, notebooks and manuscripts of works by Kharms and Vvedensky.[12] The day when they can be published in their entirety in the Soviet Union may still be far in the future. However, oblivion has been broken; a growing number of Soviet readers know about the Oberiu.

IV

What makes Daniil Kharms and Alexander Vvedensky worth reading—and worth translating—today? What are the main achievements of the Oberiuty?

As we have already seen, the Oberiuty were the last flare-up of Russian modernism before it was suffocated by Stalinist

---

[12] See n. 1, above.

socialist realism. But they also belong to the history of European literature of the absurd. They represent a high peak of artistic rejection of the old, the conventional, the traditional. They not only questioned literary conventions, but also assumptions about whatever gives stability and coherence to life and perception. The sketch "A Sonnet," by Kharms, for instance, raises doubts about memory and about words conventionally agreed upon as the basis of arithmetical number. It simply poses the question, What if one forgot which came first, 6 or 7?

A friend of Vvedensky's, a mathematician, in his everyday life exemplified the unconventionality of the group, which favored striking out along one's own line in a direction different from that taken by society and in a manner which changed fundamental ways of thinking and perceiving. He and his family referred to the main objects in their apartment by made-up proper names instead of by common nouns.

Similarly, Alexander Vvedensky expressed his distrust of conventionally accepted names and concepts. He viewed them as distractions and obstacles, rather than as aids to seeing life as it is. For example, he questioned the true nature of movement:

The names of minutes, seconds, hours, days, weeks, and months lead us away from even a superficial understanding of time. All those names are analogous either to objects or to concepts and measurements of space. For that reason, a week we have lived through lies before us like a killed deer. This would be so if time only served for the measuring of space, if this were double bookkeeping, if time were a mirror image of objects. In reality objects are a pale mirror image of time. There are no objects. Try to pick them up. A mouse is running on a rock. Count its every step. Only forget the word "every," forget the word "step." Then each of its steps will seem to be a new movement. Then as you correctly give up your perception of the series of movements as something whole that you erroneously had been calling "steps" (you confused movements and time with space), the movement will begin to crumble, it will come to almost nothing. A flickering will begin. The mouse will begin to flicker. Look around yourself: the world is flickering. Like the mouse.[13]

The emphasis on the continuity of movement and on the primacy of time over space links the Oberiuty with the Cubists, for instance with Marcel Duchamp's "Nude Descending a Staircase." It also links them in theory—just as their works often do in practice—with techniques of the film.

Like Kafka earlier and Ionesco twenty-five years later, Kharms subverts human rationality by developing its mannerisms and forms to the point of absurdity. For instance, in "Vindication" the forms are those of discursive reason at its sickest and most bitter, while the content is that of an insane mind. This short sketch recalls to us the self-justifications of Nazi prison-camp officials and reminds us of later crimes apologized for and excused by references to order, naturalness, and the needs of the state.

Kharms and Vvedensky, however (in contrast to Kafka in Austria-Hungary and Czechoslovakia, or Beckett in Ireland and France), were satirizing and parodying the monstrosities and absurdities of a special set of circumstances, of their own age, of Soviet Russia of the First Five-Year Plan and the middle 1930's. Language and rationality were being abused,

---

[13] Quoted by Alexandrov in "Oberiu," p. 299.

facts distorted, values turned upside down. Hundreds of thousands of people were being arrested, ostensibly for the purpose of creating a new, classless, perfect society.

The Leningrad black humorists produced works full of violence. They picked grotesque examples of characters who failed to react sympathetically to suffering taking place before their eyes. Their works are a comment on the grimness of life in all ages, on the lack of contact and human communication. But in addition to their timeless, universal relevance, the writings make specific comments on the concrete social and political (and hence psychological) conditions prevalent in Soviet Russia at a particular historical moment. Herein lies one point of difference between them and their Theater of the Absurd parallels in the West.

Most of Kharms's works, however, do not make as direct and explicit satirical points as those of "Vindication." Often they take an ordinary situation and reduce it to absurdity by one or several devices: nonsequitur endings (sometimes pseudo-endings or antiendings, nonconclusive conclusions) and repetitions. The last sentences of "Falling-Out Old Women" or "Blue Notebook No. 10" illustrate Kharms's quick, efficient way of disposing of a situation and his unmotivated, nonsensical endings.

In the subtitle to one of his poems, Kharms's friend Vvedensky called himself "The Auto-Rity on Nonsense," and both authors derive as much from the nonsense of Kozma Prutkov as from Edward Lear and Lewis Carroll. In their stories and plays, connections that habits of life and literature of the past have bred into us are missing. In the last line of "An Event on the Street," one Ivan Semyonovich Karpov is brought in—a man not mentioned before, about whose significance in the story we are told nothing, and the point of whose appearance is that there is no point to it. There is no rhyme or reason—this is what Kharms and Vvedensky tell us over and over. They parody the rationale of narratives with a plot, as in "Anecdotes about Pushkin's Life," which spoofs the solemn hero-worshiping stories about the celebrated poet (and about Lenin and other "serious" heroes) in which the Russians delight. The anecdotes about Pushkin, in addition, rely on the irony of the contrast between the imaginary narrator's language—impoverished clichés and untranslatable, shoddy slang expressions like "simply killing"—and the fact that the stories, with their tawdry Russian, are intended to celebrate Pushkin, who lived by and for language and was the greatest master of the Russian language.

In Kharms's narratives, things simply happen, simultaneously or seriatim. There is only a pretense of casual connection. It is a world without significance, but with a strong admixture of brutality, violence, death, and callousness.

One of Kharms's best works, the longest prose piece available to us, is "The Old Woman." (No one knows what may yet exist in manuscripts in the possession of some of his friends in Leningrad; in the manuscript collections held by the Institute of Russian Literature of the USSR Academy of Sciences, in Pushkinsky Dom in Leningrad; or elsewhere.) "The Old Woman" is a story which is a paean to ordinariness. The everyday, petty reality of Leningrad in the mid-thirties is caught as though with the lens of an accurate camera, as well as with the pen of a humorist—a humorist who is sardonic, compassionate, and resigned.

The narrator of "The Old Woman," with his writer's block, his yielding to all distractions—his finding anything more compelling than actually sitting down and writing—resembles Kharms, the speaker in the poem "I Looked for a Long Time at the Green Trees." The story exists on two levels: that of unglossed-over Soviet actuality, where it is quite natural for a passenger in a train not to put down a suitcase when going either to the conductress or to the men's room, since the suitcase will likely be stolen; and that of magic, of fantasy, where dead people crawl (or appear to crawl) and where sane persons tell stories of dead people who bite expectant mothers.

The conversation between the narrator and the character Sakerdon Mikhailovich (and many other similar passages) is utterly ordinary; everything is typical, conventional, trite, stereotyped. In such passages Kharms is writing an antistory—an apotheosis of the ordinary—a reduction of "fiction" to the dreariest, most ordinary reality, to nonfiction. The most uneventful events are noted (such as shopping and drinking vodka with a friend) and the most common ritual words that accompany these activities. But at the same time as these nonevents, occur fantastic (supernatural or magical) events. The ordinary and extraordinary, the sane and insane, the dreaming and waking states are juxtaposed.

The rapid shifting among various orders of reality is enhanced by frequent switches between the past and the present tense. The confusion of sanity and insanity leads the reader to expect eccentricity. For example, when Sakerdon jumps up and tears down a curtain, we think he is acting insanely. But his action turns out to be quite rational and even practical: enamel has cracked off a pan into which he has forgotten to put water, and he needs the curtain to use as a pot holder.

There are two additional tones or modes in the story: of zany comedy, and of religion, whose resonances we feel behind the story because of the concluding prayer. Little slips made by the narrator give rise to macabre humor; he first is afraid of being bitten by a dead woman, then remembers that she cannot bite him—not because she is dead, but because she had lost her dentures. Kharms is the chronicler and the troubadour of the trivial, the everyday, the normal, the nonevent—side by side with evocations of the magical and the zany.

Kharms and Vvedensky work out in experimental, painful, black-humor situations what might happen if certain kinds of continuities and links between items of experience (memory, for example, in "A Sonnet") vanished, or if the basis for certain assumptions we make firmly, albeit automatically and unconsciously, disappeared. Their attitude toward that fundamental fabric of patterns which give reliability and constancy to our world is the opposite of the presupposition of Henry Thoreau:

If we knew all the laws of Nature, we should need only one fact, or the description of one actual phenomenon, to infer all the particular results at that point. Now we know only a few laws and our result is vitiated, not, of course, by any confusion or irregularity in Nature, but by our ignorance of essential elements in the calculation.[14]

14 *Walden* (New York, 1942), p. 194.

Among the Oberiuty's chief interests were folk tales, Russian puppet shows, and a type of performance called a *balagan* (folk show). The quick repetitive strokes of action, the violence—fighting, hitting, and beating—and the lack of elaboration or analysis of motives or depiction of background or subtle nuances all suggest basic, folk forms of storytelling and play acting. In addition, Kharms supplies absurd twists; he wrenches things askew. The repetitions without variation, occasionally streaking into absurd denouements, are similar to devices in Beckett's *Endgame*.

Some stories, stripping away everything until less than a skeleton of a narrative is left, anticipate the recent development of minimal art in painting and sculpture. "Petrakov" and "A Meeting" could be called minimal stories; we might even claim that if Dostoevsky, in his *Notes from the Underground,* in 1864 invented, and coined the term for, the antihero, then Kharms invented the antistory in 1930, in the two brief works just named. These stories assume an air of simplicity, artlessness—a deliberate childishness. They use Gogolian nonsequiturs and elaborations of subordinate points, going off at tangents. There is much conspicuous pointlessness in them.

Some of Kharms's ideas recall to us later theatrical devices. The nausea and vomiting in "An Unsuccessful Show," for instance, are suggestive of the Living Theatre's 1969 skit in which a line of actors do nothing but clear their throats in a long series of louder and louder grunts. Some of Kharms's series of actions get out of hand: "The Carpenter Kushakov" deliberately presents a quite improbable number of fractures. Kharms exploits contrasts between the fantasticality of an extraordinary event (e.g., the falling out of the hair in "Symphony No. 2") and the utter ordinariness of all the rest of the story.

Many of Kharms's narratives are basically a working out of a simple hypothetical supposition; they are "What if" stories. What if a woman died in one's apartment? What if one forgot the proper sequence of numbers? What if one became blind and then regained one's sight? What if one kept falling down and getting hurt? The doors of potentiality are opened— a mixture of the everyday world as we know it with a world of what might happen. Conventional, typical, cause-and-effect sequences, the probabilities of everyday life are maintained; all the odds as we know them are there, but inserted among them at the outset is one incongruous (and key) element— usually an unexpected one. Kharms likes to see what consequences will develop from this kind of elaboration from a most improbable starting point in the most probable manner.

Kharms's poetry is entirely different from his prose. It combines individual clauses and phrases into a patchwork which does not make rational, sustained sense, but the connotations create an atmosphere. We cannot make our way through the poems rationally, but we feel recurrent moods: often sadness, sometimes the gaiety of children's play. Half or whole lines which make sense by themselves follow each other in what seems an almost random order. They sound as if they could be sentences or statements, but they are not. The syntax is conventional; there are clauses and the usual parts of speech, but the connections between them are mysterious or at best half-revealed. There are striking images; the mood is strong. Because the poems are almost untranslatable, they

are not included in this volume. They are to be included in the
Russian edition. Some of them remind the reader of Kharms's
favorite English author, Edward Lear.

A group of poems written in the late 1930's stands apart.
In them Kharms made straightforward statements which
resemble prose. They usually refer to elements of dreary,
repetitive daily existence—mud, dirt, broken bottles, drunken
men. We feel in them a deep-seated weariness, interrupted by
brief but poignant stabs of love and spiritual victory over
sordid everyday life. Statements such as "But I write a poem
to Natasha" appear as affirmations of a momentary victory
through poetry (creation) over a depressing physical
environment. The expression of faith in a reawakening of
"intense life" in the poem "I Looked for a Long Time at the
Green Trees" is such a moment.

One of the high points of Kharms's literary achievement is
the play "Elizabeth Bam." The basic framework (the
besieging of Elizabeth, her ignorance of what her guilt is
supposed to be, the repetition of the first scene in the final
scene) is strongly reminiscent of Kafka, as is the nightmarish,
surprising intervention of her own mother at the end; the
mother takes the side of Elizabeth's accusers and persecutors,
insanely accuses Elizabeth of murder, and asks for her arrest.
Much of the rest (Elizabeth's turning the two prosecutors
against each other and playing tricks on them, the disjointed
bickering, the storytelling, the skits and vaudeville scenes, the
fluctuating identity of characters, the songs, dances, fights,
medieval jousting, and other helter-skelter activity) is rather
like the work of the Dadaists—gay, varied, incongruous.
Unlike the Dadaists, however, the Oberiuty did not intend to

destroy art. Rather, they wished to create a new art, repudiating the conventions of previous literature.

"The Oberiu Manifesto" gives a very good account of the ideas behind "Elizabeth Bam." In contrast to many theoretical programs which differ vastly from actual practice, the Oberiu statement of theory and the play that was declared to be its exemplification are in fact excellent commentaries on each other. The Oberiuty put stress on "the concrete object cleansed of its literary and everyday shell." Their manifesto emphasizes collision and conflict. It foreshadows the French *nouveau roman* of the post–World War II era in rejecting experiences and emotions. It pays attention to atmosphere rather than plot. In "Elizabeth Bam," chaos, absurdity, and nonsense predominate, and there is sharp alternation of slapstick and pathos, merriment and anxiety. The general thrust is against psychologizing, subjective analysis, plot, and rational coherence, and toward hard-contoured delineation of individual incidents, concrete small actions, sharp junctures— not connection, modulation, transition, but shock, contrast, disjointed jumping from one element to another.

Vvedensky's "Christmas at the Ivanovs' " is funnier and even more absurd than "Elizabeth Bam." We first encounter absurdity in the contrast between the title and the list of characters. The play is called "Christmas at the Ivanovs'," but the brothers and sisters all have different surnames, and nobody, not even the parents, is called Ivanov. The seven "children" range in age from the one-year-old boy Petya Perov to Dunya Shustrova, an eighty-two-year old "girl." (The list of characters explicitly calls each of the "children" a "boy" or a "girl," although one of the "boys" is seventy-six and another twenty-five, and the "girls" are eight, seventeen, thirty-two, and eighty-two). The one-year-old boy, Petya, who is able to speak beautifully, turns out to be the wise commentator on some of the events of the play. (To be sure, in the world of this play even the body of murdered Sonia is capable of exchanging remarks with her severed head.)

The play makes fun of dramatic conventions. For example, a character uses conspicuous exposition when he says, "No, you don't know what I am about to tell you. I have a fiancée. She works . . ." The author leads us on with sentimental rhetoric, and cuts it off harshly. The play forces on us brutal horrors mixed with facetiousness.

The explicit sexual references and incidents of the play are surprising, especially in the context of normally reticent Soviet literature. The play is intended both to amuse and to shock us. It also raises the question of who is mad, who is sane: the head psychiatrist is obviously a raving lunatic; and the parents of the murdered girl, who wail about her death but at the same time undress and proceed to make love on a couch immediately beside the coffin holding their murdered daughter's severed head and body, suggest in exaggerated form the hypocrisy of banal expressions of parental grief.

This play spoofs the clichés of Christmas spirit and deserves to be produced at the proper time of year by every anti-Christmas theatrical company in the world. Vvedensky's anti-Christmas antiplay is his most hilarious as well as his most upsetting work.

He also wrote shorter plays, and many poems, the best of which is "An Elegy." He wrote a number of philosophical poems, some archaic in style and often dealing with death, and semipoetic conversations about such topics as memory and the loss of memory.

Kharms and Vvedensky employ various modes of logic and illogic. Giving free rein to the detail, to the disjointed part, they like to exploit what the collisions of elements yield in the way of shock, upset, and laughter. Elements which are found joined in coherent schemes in other authors are separated and made to clash by Kharms and Vvedensky. Their children's stories veer toward adult literature; their stories and plays for adults resemble literature for children and the writings of the insane. The two Russians share some features with Western Surrealists. Reality and unreality are mixed. The aim is to produce strong impressions of conflict, chaos, and humor. No wonder Kharms once declared that only two things in life are of great worth: humor and saintliness.

MINI-STORIES
by Daniil Kharms

The Cashier

Masha found a mushroom, picked it, and brought it to the
market. At the market someone punched Masha on the head
and told her he would kick her in the legs, too. Masha became
frightened and ran away. Masha ran to the co-op and wanted
to hide behind the cash register. The manager saw Masha and
asked, "What do you have there in your hands?" And Masha
said, "A mushroom." The manager said, "Aren't you a sharp
one! Do you want me to fix you up with a job?" Masha said,
"You won't." The manager said, "I will, too," and he fixed her
up with the job of running the cash register.

Masha kept running the register, and suddenly she died. A
militiaman came, wrote it all down, and ordered the manager
to pay a fifteen-ruble fine.

The manager asked, "Why should I pay a fine?" The
militiaman said, "For murder." The manager became
frightened, quickly paid the fine, and said, "Take this dead
cashier away as quickly as possible." The salesclerk from the
fruit department said, "No, that's not true; she was not the
cashier. She only turned the handle on the cash register. The
cashier is sitting over there." The militiaman said, "We don't
care. We've been told to carry away the cashier, and we will
carry her away." The militiaman went up to the cashier. The
cashier lay down on the floor behind the cash register and said,

"I'm not going." The militiaman asked, "Why won't you come, you fool?" The cashier said, "You are going to bury me alive."

The militiaman started to lift the cashier off the floor but could not lift her up, because the cashier was very fat. "Pull her out by her feet," said the salesclerk from the fruit department.

"No," said the manager, "this cashier is sort of like my wife. So I ask you not to pull her clothes off down below."

The cashier said, "Do you hear? Don't dare to pull my clothes off down below."

The militiaman picked up the cashier under her arms and dragged and threw her out of the co-op.

The manager ordered the salesclerks to clean up the store and to start doing business.

"And what are we to do with the dead woman?" asked the salesclerk from the fruit department, pointing at Masha.

"My God," said the manager, "we got everything mixed up. Really, what should we do with the dead woman?"

"Who will sit behind the cash register?" asked the salesclerk. The manager clutched his head. With his knee he knocked apples all over the counter and said, "This is terrible."

"This is terrible," the salesclerks said all together.

Suddenly the manager stroked his mustache and said, "Ho, ho. It is not so easy to stump me. We'll put the dead woman at the cash register; maybe the public won't figure out who it is that is sitting behind the cash register."

They put the dead woman behind the cash register, stuck a cigarette between her teeth so she would look more like a live woman, and for the sake of verisimilitude put a mushroom in her hand.

The dead woman sat behind the cash register as though she was alive; only the color of her face was very green, and one eye was open and the other completely shut.

"That's all right," said the manager; "she will do."

The public was knocking at the door and getting excited. Why was the co-op not opening up? One woman especially, in a silk coat, started shouting and shaking her bag, and aimed her heel at the door handle. Behind her an old woman with a pillowcase on her head shouted, swore, and called the manager of the co-op a scoundrel.

The manager opened the door and let the public in. The people right away ran into the meat department and then to where the sugar and pepper are sold. The old woman went at once to the fish department but on the way looked up at the cashier and stopped.

"Oh," she said, "may the Lord bless us!"

The woman in the silk coat had already been in all the departments and headed for the cash register. But as soon as she looked at the cashier, she stopped, stood silently, and stared. The salesclerks also were silent and stared at the manager. The manager looked up from behind the counter and waited to see what would happen next.

The woman in the silk coat turned to the salesclerks and asked, "Who is that sitting behind your cash register?"

The salesclerks were silent because they didn't know what to answer.

The manager was also silent.

People gathered from all directions. There was a crowd in the street. Doormen appeared. Whistles were heard. In a word, a real sensation.

The crowd was all set to stand around the co-op until nightfall. But somebody said that in Lamp Lane an old woman was falling out of the window. So the crowd at the co-op thinned out, because many people went over to Lamp Lane.

Fedya Davydovich

Fedya slowly sneaked up to the butter dish and finally seizing a moment when his wife was bending over to cut her toenails, he quickly, in one movement, slipped all the butter out of the butter dish with his finger and put it into his mouth. As he was closing the butter dish, Fedya inadvertently made a noise with the lid. His wife immediately drew herself up, and seeing the empty butter dish, pointed to it with the scissors and said severely: "There is no butter in the butter dish. Where is it?"

Fedya looked surprised and, stretching his neck, looked into the butter dish.

"The butter is inside your mouth," said his wife, pointing with her scissors at Fedya.

Fedya shook his head to say no.

"Aha," said his wife, "you are silent and you twist your head, because your mouth is packed full of butter."

Fedya bulged his eyes and waved his arms at his wife, as though to say, "What are you saying? Not at all." But his wife said, "You are lying. Open your mouth."

"Um, um, um," said Fedya.

"Open your mouth," his wife repeated.

Fedya spread his fingers wide and mumbled something, as though to say, "Oh, my, yes, I forgot, I'll be right back," and got up to leave the room.

"Stop!" his wife shouted.

But Fedya speeded up and disappeared out the door. His wife rushed after him, but she stopped at the door because she was naked, and in that state she could not go out into the hall where other occupants of the apartment walked around.

"He's gone," said his wife, sitting down on the couch. "Hell!"

Fedya went along the hall as far as a door on which hung a sign that said, "Entrance Strictly Forbidden," opened the door, and went into the room.

The room he entered was narrow and long, with the window covered by newspaper. At the right, against a wall, stood a dirty broken couch, and near the window was a table made from a board, one end of which was placed on the night table and the other on the back of a chair. On the wall at the left hung a double shelf on which was an indefinite something.

There was nothing else in the room, unless one counts a man lying on the couch, with a pale green face, dressed in a long ragged brown coat and black nankeen trousers, out of which stuck clean washed feet. This man was not sleeping, and he stared intently at the man who entered.

Fedya bowed, scraped his feet, and taking the butter out of his mouth, showed it to the man who was lying down.

"One ruble fifty," the man said without changing his position.

"Too little," said Fedya.

"Enough," said the man.

"Well, all right," said Fedya, and slipping the butter from his finger, put it on the shelf.

"Come to get the money tomorrow morning," the man said.

"What!" shouted Fedya. "I need it now. Only one ruble fifty!"

"Get out," the man said sharply, and Fedya ran out of the room on tiptoe, closing the door behind him carefully.

The Beginning of a Beautiful Day
(A Symphony)

The rooster had hardly crowed when Timofey jumped out of
the window onto the roof and frightened all the passers-by
who were on the street at that hour. The peasant Khariton
stopped, picked up a stone, and threw it at Timofey. Timofey
disappeared somewhere. "That is a clever one!" the herd of
people shouted, and Zubov ran full speed and rammed his
head into a wall. "Oh!" a woman with a swollen cheek shouted.
But Komarov beat up the woman, and the woman ran howling
through the doorway. Fetelyushin walked past and laughed
at them. Komarov walked up to him and said, "Hey, you
greaseball," and hit Fetelyushin in the stomach. Fetelyushin
leaned against the wall and started to hiccup. Romashkin spat
from the top-story window, trying to hit Fetelyushin. At that
moment, not far from there, a big-nosed woman was beating
up her kid with a trough. A fattish young mother rubbed a
pretty little girl's face against the brick wall. A little dog broke
its thin leg and rolled around on the pavement. A little boy
ate some kind of loathsome thing out of a spittoon. At the
grocery store there was a long line for sugar. The women
swore loudly and pushed one another with bags. The peasant
Khariton got drunk on denatured alcohol and stood in front of
the women with unbuttoned trousers and said bad words.

Thus began a beautiful summer day.

Symphony No. 2

Anton Mikhailovich spat, said "Ugh," spat again, said "Ugh" again, spat again, said "Ugh" again, and went out. The hell with him. I'd better tell you about Ilya Pavlovich.

Ilya Pavlovich was born in 1893 in Constantinople. When he was still a small boy, they moved to Petersburg, and there he graduated from the German School on Kirochnaya Street. Then he had a job in some kind of store; then he did something else; and when the Revolution started, he emigrated. Well, the hell with him. I'd better tell you about Anna Ignatievna.

But it is not so easy to tell you about Anna Ignatievna. First of all, I know almost nothing about her, and secondly, I have just fallen off my chair and forget what I was going to say. So I'd better tell you about myself.

I am tall, fairly intelligent; I dress meticulously and in good taste; I don't drink, I don't go to the races, but I like ladies. And ladies don't dislike me. They like it when I go out with them. Serafima Izmaylovna invited me to her place more than once, and Zinaida Yakovlevna also said that she was always glad to see me. But a funny thing happened to me with Marina Petrovna that I want to tell you about. An absolutely ordinary thing, but an amusing one. Because of me, Marina Petrovna lost all her hair—bald as the palm of your hand. It happened this way: once I went to see Marina Petrovna, and bang! she lost all her hair. That was all.

An Unsuccessful Show

(Petrakov-Gorbunov comes on the stage, wants to say something, but hiccups. He starts to vomit. He exits. Enter Pritykin.)

PRITYKIN: Petrakov-Gorbunov had to . . . *(He vomits and runs away.)*

(Makarov enters.)

MAKAROV: Egor . . . *(He runs away.)*

(Serpukhov enters.)

SERPUKHOV: So as not to be . . . *(He vomits and runs away.)*

(Kurova comes out.)

KUROVA: I should . . . *(She runs away.)*

(A little girl comes out.)

LITTLE GIRL: Daddy asked me to tell you that the theater is closing. We all feel sick.

Curtain

The Carpenter Kushakov

Once upon a time there lived a carpenter. His name was Kushakov. Once he walked out of his house and went to a store to buy carpenter's glue.

There was a thaw, and the street was very slippery. The carpenter took a few steps, slipped, fell, and broke his forehead. "Ugh," said the carpenter, got up, went to the drugstore, bought a bandage, and fixed up his forehead.

But when he walked out onto the street and took a few steps, he slipped again, fell, and broke his nose.

"Phoo!" said the carpenter, went into the drugstore, bought a bandage, and pasted his nose together with the bandage.

Then he walked out again onto the street; again he slipped; he fell and broke his cheek.

Again he had to go in the drugstore and fix up his cheek with a bandage.

"You know," the druggist said to the carpenter, "you fall so often and hurt yourself, I advise you to buy several bandages."

"No," said the carpenter, "I'm not going to fall any more." But when he walked out onto the street, he slipped again, fell, and broke his chin.

"Lousy ice!" the carpenter shouted and again ran into the drugstore.

"You see," said the druggist, "you fell down again."

"No," shouted the carpenter. "I don't want even to hear about it. Give me a bandage, quick."

The druggist gave him a bandage. The carpenter bandaged up his chin and ran home.

At home they didn't recognize him and didn't let him into his apartment.

"I am the carpenter Kushakov," the carpenter shouted.

"You don't say!" the people in the apartment answered, and bolted the door and put on the chain.

The carpenter Kushakov stood for a moment on the stairs, spat, and went out to the street.

Blue Notebook No. 10

There was once a red-haired man who had no eyes and no ears. He also had no hair, so he was called red-haired only in a manner of speaking.

He wasn't able to talk, because he didn't have a mouth. He had no nose, either.

He didn't even have any arms or legs. He also didn't have a stomach, and he didn't have a back, and he didn't have a spine, and he also didn't have any other insides. He didn't have anything. So it's hard to understand whom we're talking about.

So we'd better not talk about him any more.

Falling-Out Old Women

An old woman fell out of a window because she was too curious. She fell and broke into pieces.

Another old woman leaned out the window and looked at the one that had broken into pieces, but because she was too curious, she also fell out of the window—fell and broke into pieces.

Then a third old woman fell out of the window, then a fourth, and then a fifth.

When the sixth old woman fell out of the window, I became fed up with watching them and went to the Maltsevsky Market, where they said a blind man had been presented with a knit scarf.

An Event on the Street

Once a man jumped out of a streetcar, but so clumsily that he fell under an automobile.

Traffic on the street stopped, and a policeman tried to find out how the accident had happened.

The driver was explaining something for a long time, pointing with his finger at the front wheels of the automobile. The policeman felt the wheels with his hand and wrote the name of the street in his little book.

A fairly large crowd gathered round.

A man with dim eyes kept falling off the policeman's stand all the time.

A woman kept looking around all the time at another woman, who in her turn kept looking around all the time at the first woman.

Then the crowd dispersed and traffic started moving again.

The citizen with the dim eyes kept on falling off the stand for a long time, but in the end he, too, clearly despairing of getting himself securely seated on the policeman's stand, simply lay down on the sidewalk. At that moment a man who was carrying a chair fell down hard, under the streetcar.

A policeman came again; again a crowd gathered, and traffic stopped. The man with the dim eyes again started falling off the policeman's stand. Well, and then everything became all right, and even Ivan Semyonovich Karpov went into a restaurant.

A Sonnet

An amazing thing happened to me: I suddenly forgot which came first, 7 or 8.

I went to my neighbors and asked them what they thought about that.

I was really amazed when they told me that they too couldn't remember the counting sequence. They remembered 1, 2, 3, 4, 5, and 6, but they forgot what came after that.

We all went into the grocery store at the corner of Znamensky and Basseynaya streets and asked the cashier. The cashier smiled sadly, took a tiny little hammer out of her mouth, and slightly twitching her nose, said, "I think 7 comes after 8 in those cases when 8 comes after 7."

We thanked the cashier and ran joyfully out of the store. But then, thinking over the cashier's words, we again fell silent, because her words turned out to make no sense.

What were we to do? We went into the summer park and counted trees. But after we reached 6, we stopped and argued. Some thought 7 came next, and others that 8 came next.

We argued for a long time, but fortunately a little boy fell off a park bench and broke both jaws. This distracted us from our argument.

Then we all went home.

Vindication

I don't want to boast. But when Volodya hit me in the ear and spat in my eyes, I let him have it in a way he will never forget. It was then that I beat him with the little gas stove; yesterday I beat him with the flatiron. So he did not die right away. And where is there any proof that I cut off his leg that day? He was still alive. And I beat Andryusha to death only because I was carried away by my momentum. I am not at all responsible for that. Why did Andryusha and Liza Antonovna come in there? Who was forcing them to come in that door?

I've been accused of being bloodthirsty. It's been said I drank the blood. That is a lie. I only lapped up the puddles and the spots. It's natural to want to wipe out the traces of even the most innocent transgression. And I did not rape Liza Antonovna. First of all, she was not a virgin any more. Secondly, I was dealing with a corpse. So the accusation is beside the point. So what if she was about to have a baby! I took the child out of her. And if it wasn't capable of living, that's not my fault. I did not tear off its head. It's the fault of that thin neck. It was simply unfit for life. It's true I stomped on the dog. But it's simply cynical to accuse me of murdering a dog, when right alongside it, three human lives had been lost. I'm not counting the baby. Let us say, and I might even agree, that there was a certain amount of cruelty on my part. But to try me because I defecated on those victims is, if you pardon me, absurd. Defecating is a natural human need. So how can it be something indecent? I do understand certain fears my defense attorney has, but I believe I shall be completely vindicated.

A Meeting

The other day a man went to work, but on his way, he met another man, who had bought a loaf of Polish bread and was on his way home, to his own place.

That's about all.

Incidents

Once Orlov ate too many ground peas and died. Krylov found out about it and died too. Spiridonov up and died all by himself. Spiridonov's wife fell off the cupboard and also died. Spiridonov's children drowned in the pond. Grandma Spiridonov took to drink and hit the road. Mikhailov stopped combing his hair and caught a skin disease. Kruglov drew a picture of a lady with a whip in her hand and lost his mind. Perekhrestov was sent four hundred rubles by telegram and put on such airs that they fired him at his office.

Good people, but they don't know how to take themselves in hand.

Petrakov

The other day Petrakov wanted to go to bed, but he missed the bed and plopped down beside it. He bumped the floor so hard that he lay on the floor and couldn't get up.

So Petrakov gathered himself together and with all his strength pulled himself up on all fours. But his strength gave out, and he fell down again on his stomach and lay there.

Petrakov lay on the floor for five hours. At first he simply lay there; then he fell asleep.

Sleep put strength into Petrakov. He woke up feeling perfectly fine, got up, walked around the room, and lay down carefully on his bed. "Well, now I'll sleep," he thought. But he didn't feel like sleeping any more. He turned from side to side and couldn't fall asleep at all.

That's about all.

A Lynching

Petrov is on horseback and, turning to the crowd, makes a speech about what will happen if in place of the public park there is built an American-style skyscraper. The crowd listens and evidently agrees. Petrov writes something in his notebook. Out of the crowd comes a man of medium height who asks Petrov what he wrote in his little notebook. Petrov answers that that's his own business. The man of medium height insists. One word leads to another, and an argument starts. The crowd takes the side of the man of medium height, and to have his life Petrov urges on his horse. He hides beyond a turn in the road.

The crowd gets excited, and for lack of another victim seizes the man of medium height and tears off his head. The torn-off head rolls along the pavement and gets stuck in the drain. . . .

The crowd, having satisfied its passions, disperses.

Losing Things

Andrey Andreevich Myasov bought a wick at the market and carried it home.

Along the way Andrey Andreevich lost the wick and went into a store to buy 150 grams of Poltava sausage. Then Andrey Andreevich went to a dairy store and bought a bottle of yogurt; then he drank a small mug of kvas at a counter and waited in line to buy a newspaper. The line was quite long, and Andrey Andreevich spent about twenty minutes waiting in it, but when he got to the paper boy, he had just sold the last newspaper right in front of his nose.

Andrey Andreevich stood around for a while, then left for home, but on the way he lost the yogurt, went into a bakery, bought a French roll—but lost the Poltava sausage.

Then Andrey Andreevich went directly home, but along the way he fell down, lost the French roll, and broke his pince-nez.

Andrey Andreevich came home angry and right away went to bed to sleep, but he couldn't fall asleep for a long time, and when he did fall asleep, he had a dream: he dreamed that he had lost his toothbrush and was cleaning his teeth with some kind of candle holder.

What They Sell in
the Stores Nowadays

Koratygin came to Tikakeev's and didn't find him at home. Tikakeev just then was at the store and bought sugar, meat, and cucumbers. Koratygin hung around Tikakeev's door and was about to write him a note, when he looked and saw Tikakeev carrying an oilcloth bag in his hand.

Koratygin saw Tikakeev and shouted to him, "I've been waiting for you a whole hour."

"That's not true," said Tikakeev; "I was only gone for twenty-five minutes."

"I don't know about that," Koratygin said, "but I've been here for a whole hour."

"Don't lie," said Tikakeev. "It's a shame to lie."

"My dear sir," said Koratygin, "will you please take the trouble to choose your expressions carefully?"

"I think . . .," Tikakeev was about to say, but Koratygin interrupted him. "If you think . . .," he said, but here Tikakeev interrupted Koratygin and said, "You are a fine guy yourself."

These words so enraged Koratygin that he squeezed one of his nostrils with a finger and from his other nostril blew his nose at Tikakeev.

Tikakeev took a big cucumber out of his bag and hit Koratygin with it over the head.

Koratygin clutched his head, fell down, and died. That's how big the cucumbers are that they sell in the stores nowadays.

Anecdotes about Pushkin's Life

1

Pushkin was a poet, and all the time he was writing something. Once Zhukovsky found him writing and shouted at him, "You really are a scribbler!"

From that time on, Pushkin loved Zhukovsky and in friendly fashion called him simply Zhukov.

2

As is known, Pushkin could never grow a beard. This bothered him a lot, and he always envied Zakharyn, who on the contrary really had a properly growing beard. "His grows and mine doesn't grow," Pushkin often complained, pointing at Zakharyn with his fingernails. And each time he was right.

3

Once Petrushevsky broke his watch and sent for Pushkin. Pushkin came, looked at Petrushevsky's watch, and put it back on the chair. "What do you say, Brother Pushkin?" Petrushevsky asked. "The wheels stopped going round," Pushkin said.

4

When Pushkin broke his legs, he got about on wheels. His friends liked to tease Pushkin and caught the wheels. Pushkin became angry and wrote poems in which he swore at his friends. He called these poems "erpigarms."

5

Pushkin spent the summer of 1829 in the country. He would get up early in the morning, drink a pitcher of milk, and run to the river to bathe. After bathing in the river, Pushkin would lie down on the grass and sleep till lunch. After lunch Pushkin would sleep in his hammock. When he met smelly peasants, Pushkin would nod to them and hold his nose with his fingers. The smelly peasants would take off their caps and say, "It's nothing."

6

Pushkin loved to throw rocks. As soon as he saw a rock, he would throw it. Sometimes he became so excited that he stood, all red in the face, waving his arms, throwing rocks, simply something awful.

7

Pushkin had four sons, all idiots. One didn't even know how to sit on a chair and fell off all the time. Pushkin himself also sat on a chair rather badly. It was simply killing: they sat at the table; at one end, Pushkin kept falling off his chair continually, and at the other end, his son. Simply enough to make one split one's sides with laughter.

An Optical Illusion

Semyon Semyonovich, having put on his glasses, looks at a pine tree and sees that a peasant is sitting in the pine tree and shaking his fist at him.

Semyon Semyonovich, having taken off his glasses, looks at the pine tree and sees that nobody is sitting in the pine tree.

Semyon Semyonovich, having put on his glasses, looks at the pine tree and again sees that a peasant is sitting in the pine tree and shaking his fist at him.

Semyon Semyonovich, having taken off his glasses, again sees that nobody is sitting in the pine tree.

Semyon Semyonovich, having put on his glasses again, looks at the pine tree again, sees that a peasant is sitting in the pine tree and is shaking his fist at him.

Semyon Semyonovich doesn't want to believe in this phenomenon and decides it is an optical illusion.

A Suite

Since a long time ago, people have been reflecting on what intelligence and stupidity are. With respect to this, I remember an incident. When my aunt gave me a desk, I said to myself, "I'll sit down at the desk, and the first idea I'll come up with at that desk will be an especially intelligent one." But I wasn't able to think up an especially intelligent idea. Then I said to myself, "Very well. I didn't succeed in thinking up an especially intelligent idea, so I'll think up an especially stupid one." But I wasn't able to think up an especially stupid idea, either.

It is very difficult to do anything extreme. It is easier to do something in the middle. The center requires no effort. The center is equilibrium. There's no struggle there.

A Young Man Who
Astonished a Watchman

"Well!" said the watchman, examining the fly. "If one put carpenter's glue on it, it might be all done for. What a thing! Just simple glue."

"Hey, you," a young man who was wearing yellow gloves shouted at the watchman.

The watchman understood immediately that it was he who was being spoken to, but he went on looking at the fly.

"What do they call you?" the young man shouted again. "You ox, you."

The watchman squashed the fly with his finger and said, without turning his head in the direction of the young man: "What are you yelling for? Aren't you ashamed? I hear you anyway. No need to yell."

The young man brushed off his trousers with his gloves and asked in a delicate voice, "Tell me, old man, which way to heaven?"

The watchman looked at the young man, screwed up one eye, then screwed up the other eye, then rubbed his beard, then looked at the young man once more and said, "Don't loiter around; get a move on."

"Excuse me," said the young man. "I'm on urgent business. They even have a room ready for me there."

"Fine," said the watchman; "show me your ticket."

"I don't have a ticket. They told me they would let me in without one," said the young man, looking straight at the watchman.

"Well!" said the watchman.

"So what do you say?" asked the young man. "Will you let me through?"

"All right, all right," said the watchman. "Go ahead."

"But which way should I go? Where?" the young man asked. "I don't even know the way."

"Where do you have to go?" the watchman asked and made a severe face.

The young man put his hand over his mouth and said in a very low voice, "To heaven."

The watchman leaned forward, moved his right foot so as to stand more firmly, stared at the young man, and asked sternly: "What's the matter. Are you playing the fool?"

The young man smiled, raised one of his yellow-gloved hands, waved it over his head, and suddenly disappeared.

The watchman sniffed the air. The air smelled of burned feathers.

"Oh, my, my," said the watchman; he unbuttoned his jacket, scratched his stomach, spat at the spot where the young man had stood, and slowly went into his hut.

A Dream

Kalugin fell asleep and dreamed a dream. He was sitting in some bushes, and a militiaman went past the bushes.

Kalugin woke up, scratched his mouth, and fell asleep again, and again he dreamed a dream. He was walking past some bushes, and in the bushes a militiaman was sitting and hiding.

Kalugin woke up, put a newspaper under his head so as not to make the pillow wet with his slobbering, and fell asleep again, and again he dreamed a dream. He was sitting in some bushes, and a militiaman was walking past the bushes.

Kalugin woke up, changed the newspaper, lay down, and again fell asleep. He fell asleep and again he had a dream. He was walking past some bushes, and a militiaman was sitting in the bushes.

At that point Kalugin woke up and decided to sleep no more, but immediately he fell asleep and had a dream. He was sitting behind a militiaman, and bushes were walking past.

Kalugin shouted and turned over in his bed, but he was no longer able to wake up.

Kalugin slept for four days and nights in a row, and the fifth day he woke up so thin that he had to tie his boots to his feet with twine so that they would not keep falling off.

In the bakery, where Kalugin always bought wheat bread, they didn't recognize him and slipped him bread that was half rye.

The Sanitary Commission inspected the apartment house and saw Kalugin, and declared him to be unsanitary and good for nothing, and ordered the apartment cooperative to throw Kalugin out with the trash.

They folded Kalugin in two and threw him out with the trash.

Grigoryev and Semyonov [1]

GRIGORYEV: *(Hits Semyonov in the face.)* Well, winter has started. Time to make a fire in the stove. What do you think?

SEMYONOV: I think—if we are to think seriously about your remark—that perhaps we really ought to make a fire in the stove.

GRIGORYEV: *(Hits Semyonov in the face.)* And what do you think? Is the winter this year going to be cold or warm?

SEMYONOV: Perhaps, considering that the summer was rainy, the winter will be cold. If the summer is wet, the winter is always cold.

GRIGORYEV: *(Hits Semyonov in the face.)* I never feel cold.

SEMYONOV: That is absolutely correct, what you just said. You are never cold. You have that kind of constitution.

GRIGORYEV: *(Hits Semyonov in the face.)* I'm never cold.

SEMYONOV: Ouch!

GRIGORYEV: *(Hits Semyonov in the face.)* What do you mean, ouch?

SEMYONOV: *(Holds his cheek.)* Ouch! My face hurts.

GRIGORYEV: Why does it hurt? *(With those words, hits Semyonov in the face.)*

SEMYONOV: *(Falling on a chair)* Ouch! I myself don't know why.

---

[1] In the manuscript this dialogue has no title.—Ed.

GRIGORYEV: *(Kicking Semyonov in the face)* Nothing hurts me.

SEMYONOV: I'll teach you, son of a bitch, not to pick fights. *(Tries to get up.)*

GRIGORYEV: *(Hitting Semyonov in the face)* Look, we've got a teacher here!

SEMYONOV: *(Falls on his back.)* You dirty bastard!

GRIGORYEV: Now, now, choose your words more carefully.

SEMYONOV: *(Trying to rise)* I've put up with a lot, but this is too much. Obviously, one can't get along with you peacefully. It's your own fault.

GRIGORYEV: *(Kicks Semyonov in the face.)* Just go on talking and talking. We will listen.

SEMYONOV: *(Falls on his back.)* Ouch!

A Play

SHASHKIN (*Standing in the center of the stage*): My wife has run away. What can I do? It's all the same; once she's run away, you won't get her to come back. One must be philosophical and wise and understand that anything can happen. Blessed is he who has wisdom. Kurov doesn't have wisdom, but I have. I read a book in the public library twice. It said very intelligent things about everything.

I take an interest in everything, even in languages. I can count in French and know how to say *stomach* in German: *der Magen*. That's how. Even the painter Kozlov is my friend. We drink beer together. And Kurov? He can't even tell time. He blows his nose in his hands, eats fish with a fork, sleeps with his shoes on, doesn't brush his teeth. Phooey! That's what I call a peasant. Take him into society. They'll throw you out and curse you. If you are an intellectual, don't go around with a peasant.

You can't get the better of me. If I've got to talk to a count—I talk to a count. If I have to talk to a baron—I talk to a baron. You can't even figure out right away what kind of person I am.

It's true that I know German badly, although I do know that *stomach* is *der Magen*. But if they say to me, "Der Magen findel mooey," already I don't know what it is. But Kurov doesn't even know *der Magen*. And she ran away with that kind of a dummy. You can see what she wanted! You see, she doesn't consider me a man. She says, "You have a voice like a woman." But it's not a voice like a woman but a voice like a child. A delicate voice, a child's voice, not at all a woman's voice. What a fool she is. What did she want Kurov for? The painter Kozlov says that I'm just made for a portrait.

Sleep Teases a Man

Markov took off his shoes, sighed, and lay down on the couch.
He felt like sleeping, but as soon as he shut his eyes, the
desire to sleep immediately went away. Markov opened his
eyes and reached out for a book. But sleep again attacked him,
and Markov, without having touched the book, lay down and
shut his eyes again. But as soon as he shut his eyes, sleep fled
again, and his mind became so clear that Markov could have
solved in his head algebraic problems with equations with two
unknowns.

Markov tortured himself for a long time, not knowing what
to do, to sleep or to stay awake. In the end, having tortured
himself through and through, and having come to hate himself
and his room, Markov put on his coat and hat, took a cane,
and walked outside. A fresh breeze calmed Markov. He felt
happier and wanted to go back to his own room.

When he came into his room, he felt a pleasant, tired
sensation in his body and wanted to sleep. But as soon as he
lay down on the couch and shut his eyes, sleep vanished
immediately.

Markov leaped off the couch in a rage and, without hat or
coat, rushed toward the Tauride Park.

A Fable

A certain short man said, "I'd do anything if only I could be just a little taller."

He had hardly finished saying this when he saw a witch standing in front of him.

"What do you want?" the witch asked him.

The short man stood there, and he was so frightened, he couldn't say anything.

"Well?" said the witch.

The short man stood there and said nothing. The witch disappeared.

At that point the short man started crying and biting his nails. First he bit all the nails on his fingers and then those on his toes.

Reader, think hard about this fable and you will feel pretty strange.

The Connection

Philosopher!

1. I am writing to you in answer to your letter which you are about to write to me in answer to my letter which I wrote to you.

2. A violinist bought a magnet and was carrying it home. Along the way, hoods jumped him and knocked his cap off his head. The wind picked up the cap and carried it down the street.

3. The violinist put the magnet down and ran after the cap. The cap fell into a puddle of nitric acid and dissolved.

4. In the meantime, the hoods picked up the magnet and hid.

5. The violinist returned home without a coat and without a cap, because the cap had dissolved in the nitric acid, and the violinist, upset by losing his cap, had left his coat in the streetcar.

6. The conductor of the streetcar took the coat to a secondhand shop and exchanged it there for sour cream, groats, and tomatoes.

7. The conductor's father-in-law ate too many tomatoes, became sick, and died. The corpse of the conductor's father-in-law was put in the morgue, but it got mixed up, and in place of the conductor's father-in-law, they buried some old woman.

8. On the grave of the old woman, they put a white post with the inscription "Anton Sergeevich Kondratev."

9. Eleven years later, the worms had eaten through the post, and it fell down. The cemetery watchman sawed the post into four pieces and burned it in his stove. The wife of the cemetery watchman cooked cauliflower soup over that fire.

10. But when the soup was ready, a fly fell from the wall, directly into the pot with this soup. They gave the soup to the beggar Timofey.

11. The beggar Timofey ate the soup and told the beggar Nikolay that the cemetery watchman was a good-natured man.

12. The next day the beggar Nikolay went to the cemetery watchman and asked for money. But the cemetery watchman gave nothing to the beggar Nikolay and chased him away.

13. The beggar Nikolay became very angry and set fire to the cemetery watchman's house.

14. The fire spread from the house to the church, and the church burned down.

15. A long investigation was carried on but did not succeed in determining the cause of the fire.

16. In the place where the church had stood a club was built, and on the day the club opened a concert was organized, at which the violinist who fourteen years earlier had lost his coat performed.

17. In the audience sat the son of one of those hoods who fourteen years before had knocked the cap off that violinist.

18. After the concert was over, they rode home in the same streetcar. In the streetcar behind theirs, the driver was the same conductor who once upon a time had sold the violinist's coat in a secondhand shop.

19. And so here they are, riding late at night through the city: in front, the violinist and the hood's son; and in back, the driver, the former conductor.

20. They ride along and don't know what connection there is between them, and they won't know till the day they die.

1937

From a Notebook

An old man was scratching his head with both hands. In places where he couldn't reach with both hands, he scratched himself with one, but very, very fast. And while he was doing it, he blinked rapidly.

Steam, or so-called smoke, came out of the chimney of the locomotive. A beautiful bird flew into that smoke and flew out of it rumpled and disheveled.

Khvilishevsky ate cranberries and tried not to wince. He expected everybody to say: What strength of character! But nobody said anything.

A dog could be heard sniffing at the door. Khvilishevsky squeezed a toothbrush with his hand and stuck out his eyes so as to hear better. "If the dog comes in," Khvilishevsky thought to himself, "I'll hit it right in the temple with this bone handle."

. . . Bubbles of some kind flew out of the box. Khvilishevsky left the room on tiptoe and quietly shut the door behind him. "The hell with it," Khvilishevsky said to himself. "It's none of my business what's in it. Really! The hell with it."

A fat man invented a way of losing weight. And he lost weight. Ladies besieged him and questioned him about how he had managed to lose weight. But the man who had lost weight told the ladies that losing weight looks good on men but doesn't look good on ladies and that ladies must be plump. And he was absolutely right.

THE OLD WOMAN

by Daniil Kharms

And the following conversation took place between them.

Hamsun

An old woman is standing in the courtyard and holding a wall clock in her hands. I walk past the old woman, stop, and ask her, "What time is it?"

"You look," the old woman says to me. I look and I see that the clock has no hands.

"There are no hands," I say.

The old woman looks at the face of the clock and says to me, "It's a quarter to three."

"Oh, I see. Many thanks," I say, and go away. The old woman shouts something after me, but I don't look back. I go out to the street and walk along the sunny side. The spring sun is very pleasant. I walk, screw up my eyes, and smoke my pipe. At the corner of Sadovaya Street, I run into Sakerdon Mikhailovich. We greet each other, stop and talk for a long time. I get tired of standing out in the street and invite Sakerdon to come with me to a saloon. We drink vodka, eat egg snacks with anchovies; then we say goodby, and I walk on by myself.

Suddenly I remember that I forgot to turn off the hot plate at home. This bothers me a lot. The day had started so well, and here comes the first mishap already. I should not have gone out for a walk.

I arrive home, take off my coat, pull my watch out of my
vest pocket and hang it on a nail; then I lock the door and lie
down on the sofa. I'll lie down and try to get some sleep.

Disgusting noises made by boys are coming in from the
street. I lie and think up punishments for them. What I like
best of all is to give them tetanus paralysis so they will stop
moving. Their parents drag them to their houses. They lie in
their beds and can't even eat, because their mouths will not
open. They are fed artificially. The paralysis goes away
after a week, but they are so weak that they have to stay in
bed for a whole month more. Then they gradually begin to get
better, but I give them tetanus a second time, and they
all die.

I lie on my couch with my eyes open and can't fall asleep;
I keep remembering the old woman with the clock whom
I saw today in the yard, and it seems pleasant to me that her
clock had no hands. Recently in a secondhand shop I saw
a repulsive kitchen clock on which the hands were made to
look like a knife and fork.

My God! I have not yet turned off the hot plate. I jump up
and turn it off; then I lie down again on the couch and try
to fall asleep. I shut my eyes. I'm sleepy. The spring sun shines
through the window, straight at me. I begin to feel hot. I
get up and sit down in an armchair by the window.

Now I fell sleepy, but I'm not going to sleep. I'll take paper
and pen and I'll write. I feel tremendous strength inside me. I
thought it all out yesterday. It's going to be a story about a
magician who lives in our time and does not work miracles. He
knows he is a miracle worker and can work any miracle he
wants, but he doesn't do it. They move him out of his

apartment. He knows he would need only to wave his finger and he could keep his apartment, but he doesn't do it; he moves humbly out of his apartment and lives outside of town in a barn. He is able to turn the barn into a beautiful brick house, but he does not do that; he goes on living in the barn and in the end dies without having worked one miracle in his whole life.

I sit and rub my hands with glee. Sakerdon Mikhailovich will burst with envy. He thinks I'm no longer capable of writing a work of genius. . . . Quickly, quickly to work. Away with all dreams and laziness. I'll write for eighteen hours straight.

I tremble all over with impatience. I can't figure out what I should do. I must get pen and paper, but I pick up all kinds of things, not at all the things I need. I run around the room, from the window to the table, from the table to the hot plate, from the hot plate to the table, then to the sofa, and again to the window. I'm choking on the flame which burns inside my breast. It's only five o'clock. I have all day before me, the evening and the whole night. . . .

I stand in the middle of the room. What am I thinking about? It's already twenty to six. I've got to write. I push the table toward the window and sit down by it, graph paper in front of me, my pen in my hand.

My heart is still pounding too much. My hand trembles. I'm waiting to calm down a little. I put the pen down and fill my pipe. The sun is shining straight into my eyes. I screw up my eyes and light my pipe.

A crow flies past my window. I look out the window, down onto the street, and see a man walking along the sidewalk on an artificial leg. He is making a loud noise with his leg and stick.

"So," I say to myself, and go on looking out the window.

The sun hides behind the chimney of the house across the street. The shadow from the chimney runs along the roof, crosses the street, and settles on my face. I must take advantage of the shadow and write a few words about the magician. I pick up my pen and write: "The magician was tall."

I can't write any more than that. I sit until I start feeling hungry. Then I get up and go to the cupboard where I keep food. I rummage around, but find nothing. A lump of sugar and nothing else. Somebody is knocking at the door.

"Who is there?"

Nobody answers. I open the door and see before me the old woman who this morning stood in the yard with the clock. I'm very surprised and can say nothing.

"I have come," says the old woman, and comes into my room.

I stand by the door and don't know what to do, throw the old woman out or, on the contrary, ask her to sit down. But the old woman herself goes to my armchair by the window and sits down on it.

"Shut the door and lock it," the old woman says to me.

I shut and lock the door.

"Kneel down," say the old woman. I kneel down.

But now I begin to feel the full absurdity of my position. Why am I kneeling in front of some old woman? Why is this old woman in my room, sitting in my favorite chair? Why didn't I throw the old woman out?

"Listen," I say, "what right have you to make yourself at

home in my room and to order me about? I don't at all want to be kneeling down."

"You don't need to," the old woman says. "Now you must lie down on your stomach and touch the floor with your face."

I immediately obey her command.

I see before me precisely drawn squares. Pain in my shoulder and in my right hipbone forces me to change my position. I was lying face down; now with much effort I lift myself up to my knees. All my limbs are numb and don't bend easily. I turn around and see myself in my room, kneeling in the middle of the floor. Consciousness and memory slowly return to me. One more time I look around the room, and see that someone is sitting in the chair by the window. In my room it isn't very light yet, because it must be the time of the white nights now. I look hard. Lord! Is that old woman still sitting in my chair? I stretch my neck and look. Yes, of course, it is the old woman sitting there; her head has dropped down on her chest. She must have fallen asleep.

I get up and limp over to her. The old woman's head has dropped down on her chest; her arms are hanging along the sides of the chair. I feel like grabbing this old woman and throwing her out the door.

"Listen," I say, "you happen to be in my room. I have work to do. Please, I'm asking you, please go away."

The old woman does not move. I bend over and look at the old woman's face. Her mouth is half-open, and a steel denture hangs out of her mouth. And suddenly everything becomes clear to me: the old woman has died.

A terrible feeling of annoyance seizes me. Why did she die in my room? I can't stand dead people. And now all the bother with this corpse, having to go and talk to the janitor and house superintendent, explain to them why this old woman showed up at my place. I look at the old woman with hate. Maybe she has not died. I feel her forehead. The forehead is cold. Her hand also. Well, what should I do?

I light my pipe and sit down on the sofa. An insane rage rises up in me. "What a bastard!" I say out loud.

The dead old woman sits in my chair like a sack. Her dentures stick out of her mouth. She looks like a dead horse.

"A disgusting sight," I say, but I can't cover the old woman with a newspaper, because all sorts of things can happen under a newspaper.

On the other side of the wall someone can be heard moving. My neighbor, a locomotive engineer, is getting up. All I need now is for him to find out that a dead old woman is sitting in my room. I listen to his footsteps. Why is he so slow? It's five-thirty. He should have left long ago. My God! He is starting to drink tea. I hear the noise of the primus the other side of the thin wall. Oh, if only that damned engineer would leave quickly.

I get on the couch and lie down. Eight minutes pass, but the neighbor's tea is still not ready and the primus buzzes. I shut my eyes and doze off.

I dream that my neighbor goes out and that I go out with him onto the staircase and bang the door, with the safety lock on, behind me. I don't have the key on me and can't get back into the apartment. I have to ring the bell and wake up the other tenants, and that is altogether bad. I stand on the landing and wonder what to do, and suddenly I see I have no hands. I tilt my head to see better if I have hands, and I see

that on one side, instead of a hand I have a knife, and on
the other side, a fork. "Here," I say to Sakerdon Mikhailovich,
who for some reason is also sitting there on a folding chair.
"You see," I say to him, "what kind of hands I have?"

Sakerdon Mikhailovich sits there silently, and I see it is not
the real Sakerdon Mikhailovich, but one made out of clay.

I wake up and right away believe that I am lying at home in
my room on a sofa and that the old woman is sitting in a chair
by the window.

Quickly I turn my head toward her. The old woman is not
on the chair. I look at the empty chair and wild joy fills me.
That means it was all a dream. But where did it start? Did the
old woman come into my room yesterday? Maybe that too
was a dream? I returned home yesterday because I forgot to
turn off the hot plate. But maybe that was a dream too? In any
event, how good that the old woman is not in my room now
and that I don't need to see the house superintendent and
bother him with the old woman.

But how long did I sleep? I look at my watch: half past
nine. It must be morning.

God! The things one dreams in a dream.

I drop my feet off the sofa, get ready to get up, and suddenly
I see the dead old woman, lying on the floor behind the table
alongside the chair. She was lying with her face up, and the
denture had fallen out of her mouth and one tooth was pushed
into her nostril. Her arms had twisted under her body, and
could not be seen. From under the hiked-up skirt there stuck
out bony legs in dirty white wool stockings.

"Bastard!" I shouted and, running up to the old woman,
kicked her in the chin.

The denture flew off into the corner. I wanted to kick the old woman one more time, but I got scared that the body might get marked, and then on top of everything, they would decide that I killed her.

I left the old woman, sat down on the sofa, and lit my pipe. Fifteen minutes went by. Now it became clear to me that it was all the same: they will turn the matter over to the criminal investigation department, and the dopes will accuse me of murder. A serious situation will develop, and here I had to kick her with my shoe.

I went up to the old woman again, bent over her, and examined her face. There was a little dark spot under her chin. No, there is no getting away from it. Perhaps the old woman ran into something while she was still alive? I calm down a little and start walking around the room, smoking a pipe and thinking about the situation I'm in. I even start trembling from hunger. One more time I poke around in the food cupboard, but find nothing except a lump of sugar.

I take out my billfold and count my money. Eleven rubles. That means I can buy ham sausage for myself, and bread, and there will be money left over for tobacco.

I straighten out my necktie, which had gotten messed up during the night, take my watch, put on a coat, go out into the hall, carefully shut the door of my room, put the key in my pocket, and walk out to the street. First of all I must eat something; then my head will clear up, and then I'll do something or other with that corpse.

On my way to the store something else occurs to me: Shouldn't I go to see Sakerdon Mikhailovich and tell him everything? Perhaps together we can better decide what to do.

But I reject that idea right away, because there are some things that must be done without witnesses.

In the store they didn't have pressed ham, and I bought half a kilogram of Paris sausages. They were also out of tobacco. From the store I went to the bakery.

In the bakery there was a big crowd, and a long line waited at the cash register. Immediately I became cross but stood in line anyway. The line moved very slowly, and then even stopped altogether, because there was some kind of scene taking place at the cash register.

I pretended I noticed nothing and looked at the back of a young woman who stood in line ahead of me. The woman was clearly very curious: she stretched her neck to the right and the left, and stood on tiptoe all the time so she could see better what was happening at the cash register. Finally she turned to me and asked, "You don't know what is happening there?"

"Excuse me, I don't know," I said as dryly as I could. The woman turned in various directions and finally again turned to me: "You couldn't go and find out what's happening there?"

"Excuse me, that doesn't interest me at all," I said still more dryly.

"What do you mean, doesn't interest you!" the woman shouted. "You yourself are being held up in the line because of it."

I answered nothing and bowed slightly. The lady looked at me attentively.

"Of course, it is not a man's job to stand in line for bread," she said. "I'm sorry for you. You have to stand here. You must be a bachelor."

"Yes, I'm a bachelor," I answered, a little disconcerted, but impelled to continue to answer rather dryly, bowing slightly at the same time.

The woman looked me over from head to toe once more, and then suddenly, touching my sleeve with her finger, she said, "Let me buy what you need, and you wait for me outside."

I became terribly agitated.

"Thank you," I said. "That's very nice of you, but I can do it myself."

"No, no," the woman said, "go outside. What do you want to buy?"

"You see," I said, "I was going to buy half a kilo of black bread, the cheaper kind. I like it best of all."

"Well, that's all right," said the woman. "Now go. I'll buy it, and then we'll settle the account."

She even nudged me lightly under the elbow.

I walked out of the bakery and stood right by the door. The spring sun shines right in my face. I light my pipe. What a nice woman. That is so rare nowadays. I stand there, close my eyes because of the sun, smoke my pipe, and think about the nice woman. She even has light-brown eyes. Simply delightful, how pretty she is.

"You smoke a pipe?" I hear a voice say right alongside me. The nice lady is handing me a loaf of bread.

"Thank you very, very much," I say, taking the loaf of bread.

"And you smoke a pipe? I like that tremendously," says the nice woman to me.

And the following conversation takes place between us:

SHE: You go to buy bread yourself?

I: Not only bread; I buy everything for myself.

SHE: And where do you have lunch?

I: Usually, I cook my own. Sometimes I eat in the saloon.

SHE: You like beer?

I: No, I like vodka better.

SHE: I like vodka too!

I: You like vodka? How nice. I should like to have a drink with you sometimes.

SHE: I should like to have a vodka with you.

I: Excuse me, may I ask you something?

SHE: (*Blushing strongly*) Of course; ask me.

I: Very well, I'll ask you. Do you believe in God?

SHE: (*Surprised*) In God? Yes, of course.

I: And what would you say if we went to buy some vodka now and went to my place. I live right here.

SHE: (*Eagerly*) Why not? Let's go.

I: So let's go.

We go into a store and I buy half a liter of vodka. I don't have any more bills, only some change. All the time we talk about various things, and suddenly I remember that in my room there lies on the floor a dead old woman. I look around at my new acquaintance. She is standing at the counter and examining the jars of jam. I cautiously make my way to the door and walk out of the store. Directly across from the store there is a streetcar stop. I jump into a streetcar, even without looking to see what number it is. On Mikhailovskaya Street, I get off and go to Sakerdon Mikhailovich's. I hold the bottle of vodka, the sausages, and the bread in my hands.

Sakerdon Mikhailovich himself opened the door for me. He wore a dressing gown with nothing on underneath, boots with the tops cut off, and a fur cap with ear flaps, but the ear flaps were turned up and tied in a bow at the top of his head.

"Very glad to see you," Sakerdon Mikhailovich said when he saw me.

"I'm not interrupting your work?" I asked.

"No, no," Sakerdon Mikhailovich said. "I wasn't doing anything, just sitting on the floor."

"You see," I said to Sakerdon Mikhailovich, "I brought some vodka and snacks to eat with it. If you don't mind, let's have a drink."

"Very well," Sakerdon Mikhailovich said. "Come on in."

We went into his room. I took the cork out of the vodka bottle, and Sakerdon Mikhailovich put two glasses and a plate with boiled meat on the table.

"Here are some sausages," I said. "How are going to eat them, uncooked or boiled?"

"Let's boil them," Sakerdon Mikhailovich said, "and while they are boiling let's have a drink and some boiled meat. It's soup meat, superb boiled meat."

Sakerdon Mikhailovich put a pan on the kerosene stove, and we sat down to drink vodka.

"It's healthy to drink vodka," Sakerdon Mikhailovich said, and filled our glasses. "Mechnikov has written that vodka is healthier than bread, because bread is just straw that rots in our stomachs."

"Here's to you," I said, and we clinked glasses.

We drank, and ate some cold meat.

"Tastes good," said Sakerdon Mikhailovich.

But at that moment, there was a sharp, cracking sound in the room.

"What's that?" I asked.

We sat in silence and listened. Suddenly there was the same

sound again. Sakerdon Mikhailovich jumped off his chair, ran to the window, and tore down the curtain.

"What are you doing?" I shouted.

But Sakerdon Mikhailovich, without answering me, went to the stove, used the curtain to pick up the pan, and put the pan on the floor.

"Hell!" said Sakerdon Mikhailovich. "I forgot to put water in the pan, and the pan is enameled, and now the enamel has cracked off."

"I see," I said, and nodded. We sat down again at the table.

"Hell," said Sakerdon, "we'll eat the sausage uncooked."

"I'm terribly hungry," I said.

"Eat," said Sakerdon Mikhailovich, and pushed the sausage over to me.

"The last time I ate was yesterday, with you in a saloon, and since then I haven't had anything to eat," I said.

"Hell," Sakerdon Mikhailovich shouted in an exaggerated manner, "it's nice to see a genius in front of me."

"Oh, come on," I said.

"Did you get a lot of work done?" Sakerdon Mikhailovich asked.

"Yes," I said, "I wrote an awful lot of pages."

"Here's to the genius of our day," Sakerdon Mikhailovich said, and lifted up his glass.

We drank. Sakerdon Mikhailovich ate the boiled meat, and I ate the sausages. I ate four sausages, lit my pipe, and said, "You know, I came to see you so I would escape being pursued."

"Who pursued you?" Sakerdon Mikhailovich asked.

"A lady," I said. But since Sakerdon Mikhailovich did not ask me any more questions but just silently poured a glass of vodka, I went on: "I met her in the bakery and fell in love right away."

"Is she pretty?" Sakerdon Mikhailovich asked.

"Yes," I said, "my type." We drank, and I went on: "She agreed to come to my place and have a drink of vodka. We went into a store, but I had to sneak out of the store."

"Not enough money?" Sakerdon Mikhailovich asked.

"No, I could have just squeaked by," I said, "but I remembered I couldn't let her into my room."

"Why, was there another lady in your room?" Sakerdon Mikhailovich asked.

"Yes, if you want to put it that way, there's another lady in my room," I said, and smiled. "I can't let anybody into my room right now."

"Get married. Are you going to invite me to dinner?" Sakerdon Mikhailovich said.

"No," I said, and chuckled, "I'm not going to marry the lady."

"Well, so marry the one from the bakery," Sakerdon Mikhailovich said.

"Why are you trying to marry me off?" I said.

"Well," said Sakerdon Mikhailovich, and filled the glasses. "Here's to your success."

We drank. The vodka must have started going to our heads. Sakerdon Mikhailovich took off his fur cap with the flaps and tossed it on the bed. I got up and walked around the room and already felt a little dizzy.

"What is your opinion of dead people?" I asked Sakerdon Mikhailovich.

"Very poor," Sakerdon Mikhailovich said; "I'm scared of them."

"Me, too. I can't stand dead people," I said. "If a dead person came my way, unless he was a relative of mine, I'd give him a kick with my foot."

"One shouldn't kick dead people," Sakerdon Mikhailovich said.

"I would kick him with my boot right in the puss," I said. "I can't stand dead people and children."

"Yes, children are awful," Sakerdon Mikhailovich agreed.

"And what do you think are worse: dead people or children?" I asked.

"I guess children; they bother us more often. Dead people, at any rate, don't barge into our lives," Sakerdon Mikhailovich said.

"They do barge in!" I yelled, and shut up right away. Sakerdon Mikhailovich looked at me carefully.

"Do you want some more vodka?" he asked.

"No," I said, but added in a hurry: "No, thank you, I don't want any more."

I went up to the table and sat down. We were silent for some time.

"I want to ask you something," I said finally. "Do you believe in God?"

A horizontal wrinkle appeared across Sakerdon Mikhailovich's forehead, and he spoke: "Some actions are impolite. It is impolite to ask a man to lend us fifty rubles after we have just watched him put two hundred into his pocket. He either has to lend us the money or refuse, and the most convenient and pleasant manner of refusing is to lie and say that one doesn't have the money. You saw that the man had the money and hence you deprived him of the possibility of refusing you simply and pleasantly. You deprived him of the right of choice, and that is a dirty trick. That is an impolite and tactless action. And to ask a man, 'Do you believe in God?'—that too is a tactless and impolite action."

"Why," I said, "that's quite different."

"I'm not comparing it," Sakerdon Mikhailovich said.

"All right," I said, "never mind. Just excuse me for asking you such an impolite and tactless question."

"All right," Sakerdon Mikhailovich said. "I simply refused to answer you."

"I wouldn't answer either," I said, "but for a different reason."

"What reason?" Sakerdon Mikhailovich asked weakly.

"You see," I said, "I don't think there are people who believe or who don't believe. There are only people who want to believe and people who want not to believe."

"That means that the ones who want not to believe already believe in something," Sakerdon Mikhailovich said, "and those who want to believe already, beforehand, don't believe in something?"

"Perhaps, even in mortality," I said.

"So why did you ask me if I believe in God?"

"Simply in order to ask you, 'Do you believe in mortality?' It sounds sort of stupid," I said to Sakerdon Mikhailovich, and I got up.

"What are you doing, going away?"

"Yes," I said, "it's time for me to go."

"And what about the vodka?" said Sakerdon Mikhailovich. "There is only enough left for a glass for each."

"Well, let's finish it, then," I said. We finished the vodka and ate all that was left of the boiled meat.

"Now, I've got to go," I said.

"So long," Sakerdon Mikhailovich said, and saw me through the kitchen to the stairs. "Thank you for the things you brought."

"Thank you," I said; "so long." And I left.

When he was left alone, Sakerdon Mikhailovich cleared the table, put the empty vodka bottle on the shelf, again put on his fur cap with ear flaps, and sat down on the floor below the window. Sakerdon Mikhailovich put his hands behind his back, and they disappeared from view. His naked bony feet, in Russian boots with the tops cut off, stuck out from under the ragged robe.

I walked along the Nevsky, deep in thought. I must go right now to the house superintendent and tell him everything. And after I take care of the old woman, I'll stand for days on end near the bakery until I meet that nice lady. I owe her forty-eight kopeks for the bread. I had a perfect excuse to look for her. The vodka I had drunk was still having its effect on me, and it seemed to me that everything was working out well and simply.

On the Fontanka I went up to a stall and with what change I had left I bought a big mug of bread kvas. The kvas was bad and sour, and I went on my way with a foul taste in my mouth.

At the corner of Liteyny, some drunk stumbled and bumped into me. A good thing I don't have a revolver. I would have killed him on the spot.

I must have walked all the way to the house with my face twisted with rage. In any event everybody who met me turned around to look after me.

I went into the house office. A small, dirty, one-eyed,

tow-haired girl with a turned-up nose was sitting on the table, looking into a pocket mirror and putting on lipstick.

"Where is the house superintendent?" I asked. The girl said nothing and continued to put on lipstick.

"Where is the house superintendent?" I repeated sharply.

"He'll be here tomorrow, not today," the dirty, one-eyed, tow-haired girl with the turned-up nose answered.

I walked out. Across the street the cripple with an artificial leg was walking, banging his leg and stick loudly. Six boys ran after him, making fun of the way he was walking.

I turned into the main doorway of my house and started climbing the stairs. I stopped on the second floor. A disgusting idea struck me: the old woman must be beginning to decompose. I didn't shut the windows, and people say that when a window is open, dead people decompose sooner. How stupid! And the damned house superintendent won't be home until tomorrow! I stood there indecisively for a few minutes and then went on up the stairs.

I stopped again close to the door of my apartment. Maybe I should go to the bakery and wait for the nice lady? I would beg her to let me stay at her place for two or three nights. But then I remembered that she bought bread today and so wouldn't be coming to the bakery. And anyway nothing would have come of that anyhow.

I unlocked the door and went into the hall. The light was on at the end of corridor, and Marya Vasilevna was holding some kind of rag in her hand and rubbing it with another rag. When she saw me, Marya Vasilevna shouted, "Shome kind of an old man ashked for you!"

"What kind of old man?" I asked.

"I don't know," Marya Vasilevna answered.

"When was it?" I asked.

"I don't know that either," Marya Vasilevna said.

"Did you talk with the old man?" I asked Marya Vasilevna.

"I did," Marya Vasilevna said.

"So how come you don't know when it was?" I said.

"Two hourzh ago," Marya Vasilevna said.

"What did that old man look like?" I asked.

"I don't know that either," Marya Vasilevna said, and went into the kitchen.

I went to my room.

I thought, "Suddenly the woman has disappeared. I'll go into the room and the old woman won't be there. My God, don't miracles happen sometimes?"

I unlocked the door and started to open it slowly. Maybe it only seemed so to me, but the sickly smell of the beginning of decomposition met me. I glanced past the half-open door and froze. The old woman was crawling toward me on all fours.

I banged the door shut with a shout, turned the key, and jumped to the wall across the hall.

Marya Vasilevna appeared in the hall.

"You called me?" she asked. I was shaking so that I couldn't answer anything and only shook my head to say No. Marya Vasilevna came closer.

"You were talking with shomebody," she said. I again shook my head.

"Inshane," Marya Vasilevna said, and again went into the kitchen, turning around to look back at me several times as she went.

"I can't stand here like this. I can't stand here like this," I repeated in my head. This sentence somehow sank deeper into me. I kept repeating it until it penetrated my consciousness. "Yes, I can't stand here like this," I said to myself, but went on standing there as though paralyzed. Something terrible had happened, but it was up to me to do something perhaps still more terrible. My thoughts spun round like a tornado, and I saw only the eyes of the dead old woman as she crawled toward me slowly on all fours.

I must rush into the room and smash the old woman's skull. That's what I must do! I looked around and felt happy when I saw a croquet mallet that for some unknown reason had for many years been standing in the corner of the hall. I must grab the mallet, rush into the room, and—bang!

The trembling had not yet stopped. I was standing with my shoulders hunched up from the cold inside me. My thoughts jumped around, moving into new areas, and I stood and listened to my thoughts and felt as though I was standing off to the side of them and as though I was not their commander.

My thoughts were explaining to me, "Dead people are not very nice. We say, 'Rest in peace,' but they give us no rest and peace. One must watch them and watch them. Ask any guard at the morgue. Why do you think he is there? For just one thing: to watch and watch, so the dead people won't scatter all over. Amusing incidents of that sort happen. One dead man, while the guard was in the public baths on orders from his superiors, sneaked out of the morgue and crept into the disinfecting chamber and ate up a pile of linen there. The disinfectors really beat up that dead man, but they had to pay out of their own pockets for the ruined linen. Another dead man crawled into the maternity ward and so scared the expectant mothers that one of them up and had a miscarriage, and the dead man threw himself on the miscarried fetus and started to eat it up, and slurped while he was doing it. When one brave nurse hit the dead man in the back with a stool, he bit her leg, and she died quickly of blood poisoning. Yes, dead people are not very nice, and one has to be on the lookout with them!"

"Stop!" I said to my own thoughts. "You talk nonsense. Dead people can't move about."

"Very well," my own thoughts said to me. "So go into your room, where, as you say, there is a dead person who can't move about."

I unexpectedly became stubborn.

"I will go into my room!" I said decisively to my own thoughts.

"Try it!" my own thoughts said to me mockingly.

This mockery enraged me once and for all. I picked up the croquet mallet and moved toward the door.

"Wait!" my own thoughts shouted. But I had already turned the key and swung open the door.

The old woman was lying at the threshold, with her face on the floor. I stood ready, with the mallet raised high. The old woman was not moving. My fever went away, and my thoughts flowed clearly. I was their commander.

"First, shut the door!" I commanded myself.

I took the key from the outside of the door and put it in the lock from the inside. I did this with my left hand, and with the right I held the croquet mallet and the whole time kept my eyes on the old woman. I locked the door and stepped cautiously over the old woman and walked to the middle of the room.

"Now we'll get even," I said. I came up with a plan such as murderers in crime stories and newspaper reports often resort to. I simply wanted to hide the old woman in a suitcase, take her out of town, and throw her into a marsh. I knew one such place. I had a suitcase under the ottoman. I pulled it out and opened it. Some odds and ends were in it—a few books, an old flannel hat, and ragged linen. I took all that out and laid it on the ottoman.

At that moment, the outside door banged loudly, and it seemed to me that the old woman shivered.

I jumped up and seized the croquet mallet.

The old woman was lying quietly. I stand and listen. It is the engineer who has come back; I hear him walking around in his room. He goes through the hall to the kitchen. If Marya Vasilevna tells him I acted insanely, it will be bad. What a mess. I must go to the kitchen, too, and calm both of them down.

Again I stepped across the old woman, put the mallet alongside the door, so that when I returned again I could take up the mallet before I even came into the room, and went out into the hall. Voices came from the kitchen, but I could not hear the words. I shut the door to my room behind me and carefully went toward the kitchen. I wanted to find out what Marya Vasilevna and the engineer were talking about. The engineer was talking, evidently telling about something that had happened to him at work.

I went in. The engineer stood with a towel in his hand and

talked, and Marya Vasilevna sat on a stool and listened. When he saw me, the engineer waved at me.

"Hello, hello, Matvey Filipovich," I said to him, and went to the bathroom. So far everything was quiet. Marya Vasilevna had become used to my eccentricities, and she may have forgotten the last incident.

Suddenly I had a brain storm: I had not locked my door, and what if the old woman crawled out of the room? I was going to rush back, but restrained myself in time, and walked through the kitchen calmly, so as not to frighten the tenants.

Marya Vasilevna was drumming on the table with her fingers and said to the engineer: "That's great, that's great. I would have blown the whistle, too."

Feeling tense, I went out into the hall and almost ran to my room.

Outside everything seemed quiet. I went up to the door and opened it a little and looked into the room. The old woman was lying there, quiet as before, face down on the floor. The croquet mallet stood by the door, as before. I took it, went into the room, and locked the door behind me. Yes, the room definitely smelled of a corpse. I stepped across the old woman, went up to the window, and sat down in the armchair. If only I didn't get sick from the smell, which was still only faint though unbearable. I lit a pipe. I felt a little nauseous and had a slight stomach ache. Why am I sitting here like this. I must act before the old woman does rot through and through. In any event, I must stuff her into the suitcase with care; that's exactly when she might bite my finger. To die of gangrene blood poisoning from a corpse—no, thank you.

"Ha-ha!" I suddenly shouted. "And what will you bite me with? Your teeth are over there!"

I turned around in the armchair and looked into the corner on that side of the window where, according to my reckoning, the dead woman's denture had to be. But the denture was not there.

I started to think: "Perhaps the dead old woman crawled around the room and looked for her teeth? Maybe she even found them and put them into her mouth?"

I took the croquet mallet and poked around with it in the corner. No, the denture was lost. I took a thick flannelet bed sheet out of the chest and went up to the old woman. I held the croquet mallet in my right hand, ready, and in my left hand I held the flannelet sheet.

The old woman aroused a disgusting fear in me. I raised up her head with the mallet. Her mouth was open, her eyes had rolled upward, and all over her chin, where I had hit her with the shoe, a large dark spot had spread. I looked into the old woman's mouth. No, she had not found her denture. I dropped her head. The head fell and hit the floor.

Then I spread out the flannelet sheet on the floor and pulled it right up to the old woman.

Then I turned the old woman over with my foot and the croquet mallet—over to the left and onto her back. Now she was lying on the sheet. The old woman's legs were bent at the knees, and her fists were touching her shoulders. It looked as if the old woman, lying on her back like a cat, was preparing to defend herself against an attacking eagle. The sooner the corpse is gone, the better.

I wrapped the old woman in the thick sheet and lifted her

up. She was lighter than I had thought. I eased her down into the suitcase and tried to shut the lid. I expected all sorts of difficulties, but the lid shut comparatively easily. I snapped the locks of the suitcase and stood up.

The suitcase is in front of me, looking quite respectable, as if there were linen and books inside it. I picked it up by the handle and tried to lift it. Yes, of course, it was heavy, but not too bad. I would be quite able to carry it to the streetcar.

I looked at my watch. Five twenty. Good. I sat down in the armchair to catch my breath a little and to smoke a pipe.

Evidently the sausages I ate today were not very good, because my stomach hurt more and more. Or maybe it was because I ate them uncooked? Or maybe my stomach ache was caused simply by nerves?

I sit and smoke. Minute after minute passes. The spring sun is shining through the window, and I screw up my eyes against its rays. Now it has hidden behind the chimney of the house across the street, and the shadow of the chimney runs along the roof, flies across the street, and lands on my face. I recall how yesterday at this time I was sitting and writing a story. Here is the graph paper and on it is written in a fine hand: "The magician was tall."

I looked out the window. The cripple with the artificial leg was walking along the street and knocking loudly with his leg and stick. Two workers and an old woman with her arms akimbo roared with laughter at the cripple's ridiculous way of walking.

I got up. It's time. Time to go. Time to take the old woman to the marsh. I must borrow money from the engineer.

I went into the hall and went up to his door.

"Matvey Filipovich, are you there?" I asked.

"I'm here," the engineer answered.

"Excuse me, Matvey Filipovich, do you have a lot of money? I get paid the day after tomorrow. You couldn't lend me thirty rubles?"

"I could," the engineer said. I coud hear him clanking his keys, opening some kind of box. Then he opened the door and reached out to me a new thirty-ruble note.

"Many thanks, Matvey Filipovich," I said.

"That's all right, that's all right," the engineer said. I stuck the money in my pocket and returned to my room. The suitcase stood undisturbed where it was before.

"Now, without delay, hit the road," I said to myself.

I took the suitcase and walked out of the room. Marya Vasilevna saw me carrying the suitcase and shouted, "Where are you going?"

"To my aunt's," I said.

"Are you coming back soon?" Marya Vasilevna asked.

"Yes," I said. "I only have to take some linen to my aunt's. Maybe I'll be back later today."

I walked outside. I was all right as far as the streetcar, changing the suitcase from my right hand to my left hand and back again.

I got up onto the front platform of the trailer car of the streetcar and waved to the conductress to come and collect the fare for the luggage and my ticket. I didn't want to pass my only thirty-ruble note down through the whole streetcar or to put down the suitcase and go to the conductress myself. The conductress came up to the platform to me and announced that she had no change. I had to get off at the next stop.

I stood there in a rage and waited for the next streetcar. I had a pain in my stomach, and my legs trembled slightly. Suddenly I saw my nice lady: she was crossing the street and wasn't looking in my direction.

I grabbed my suitcase and rushed after her. I didn't know her name and couldn't call her. The suitcase was a terrible nuisance. I held it in front of me with both hands and gave it little pushes with my knees and stomach. The nice lady was walking quite fast, and I felt I wouldn't catch up with her. I was all sweaty and getting weak. The nice lady turned into a little side street. When I got to the corner, she was gone.

"The damned old woman!" I hissed, and tossed the suitcase on the ground.

The sleeves of my jacket were wet through and through with sweat and stuck to my arms. I sat down on the suitcase and took out my handkerchief and wiped my neck and face. Two small boys stopped in front of me and stared at me. I put on a calm face and stared fixedly at a nearby house entrance as though I were waiting for someone. The boys were whispering to each other and pointing at me with their fingers. I was choking with a wild rage. Oh, if I could paralyze them with tetanus!

And because of those stinking little boys I got up, lifted the suitcase, walked with it to the entrance, and looked inside. I put on an impassive face, get out my watch, shrug my shoulders. The boys observe me from a distance. I shrug my shoulders once more and look inside the entrance.

"Strange," I said loudly, picked up the suitcase, and dragged it to the streetcar stop. I got to the railroad station at six fifty-five. I buy a round-trip ticket to Lisy Nos and sit down in the train.

In the car, besides me, were two other people: one looked like a worker; he was tired and had pushed his cap over his eyes and was sleeping. The other, still a young fellow, was dressed like a village dandy: under his suit jacket he wore a pink blouse; a cowlick was sticking out from under his cap. He was smoking a cigarette, which he held in a bright-green plastic cigarette holder.

I put the suitcase down between the benches and sat down. I had such stomach cramps that I clenched my fists so as not to moan with pain.

Two militiamen were leading some kind of man along the platform to the police station. He went along with his hands behind his back and his head hanging down.

The train moved. I looked at my watch: seven ten. Oh, how happily I'll drop that old woman in the marsh! Only a pity I didn't take my cane with me. I'm sure the old woman will need pushing under.

The dandy in the pink blouse started examining me insolently. I turn my back on him and look out the window. There are terrible cramps in my stomach. I clench my teeth, tighten my fists, and tense my legs.

We are passing through Lanskaya and Novaya Derevnya. The golden top of the Buddhist pagoda gleams, and there is the sea. But here I jump up and, forgetting everything around me, scamper to the toilet. I feel I'm rocking and spinning on a huge wave.

The train slows down. We are approaching Lakhta. I'm

sitting there, too scared to move, afraid that at the stop they might throw me out of the toilet.

If it would start moving! If it would start moving! The train moves, and I shut my eyes with delight. Oh, these moments are so sweet, the moments of love. I feel much stronger, but I know that a terrible decline will follow.

The train stops again. It is Olgino; again that torture.

But now a false alarm. Cold sweat rises on my forehead, and a light chill flutters around my heart. I get up and stand for some time with my head pressed against the wall. The train is moving, and the rocking of the car is pleasant. I gather all my strength together and totter out of the toilet.

There is nobody in the car. Evidently the worker and the dandy with the pink blouse got off at Lakhta or Olgino. Slowly I got to my window. Suddenly I stop and stare stupidly in front of me. The suitcase is not where I left it. It must be that I'm at the wrong window. I leap to the next window. No suitcase. I leap back, forward, I run along both sides of the car, I look under the seats, but there is no suitcase anywhere.

Can there be any doubt? Of course, while I was in the toilet, they stole my suitcase. It could have been expected. I sit on the seat with my eyes bulging, and for some reason I recall how, at Sakerdon Mikhailovich's, the enamel made a noise when it cracked away from the heated-up pan.

"What has happened?" I ask myself. Well, who will believe now that I didn't kill the old woman? They will arrest me today, here or in town at the railway station, like that man who was walking along with his head bent down.

I walk out onto the platform of the train. The train is getting close to Lisy Nos. Little white fence posts flash by. The train stops. The steps of my car don't reach to the ground. I jump down and go to the station. The train for the city will be leaving in half an hour.

I go into some little woods. There are juniper bushes. Nobody will see me behind them. I go toward them.

A large green caterpillar is crawling on the earth. I kneel down and touch it with my finger. The caterpillar winds itself up tightly and firmly several times in one direction and then in the other.

I turn around. No one can see me. A light shiver runs down my spine. I bend my head low and say in a low voice: "In the name of the Father and the Son and the Holy Ghost, now and forever and forever and ever, amen."

. . . . .

I temporarily end my manuscript here, since I think that even now it is already sufficiently drawn out.

End of May, first half of June, 1939

ELIZABETH BAM

by Daniil Kharms

(A small, deep room.)

ELIZABETH BAM: Any minute now the door will open and they'll come in. They'll certainly come in so that they can catch me and wipe me out. What have I done? What have I done? If I had only known . . . Run? Where can I run? This door leads to the stairs, and on the stairs I would run into them. Out the window? *(Looks out the window.)* Oh, it is high. I can't jump. Well, what can I do? Oh, somebody's coming. It's them. I'll lock the door, and I'll not open it. Let them knock as much as they like.

(Knocking on the door.)

VOICE: Elizabeth Bam, open up. *(Pause.)* Elizabeth Bam, open up.

VOICE FROM THE DISTANCE: Why won't she open the door?

VOICE BEHIND THE DOOR: She will open. Elizabeth Bam, open up!

FIRST VOICE: Elizabeth Bam, I order you to open immediately.

SECOND VOICE: *(Low)* Tell her otherwise we'll break the door down. Let me try.

FIRST VOICE: *(Loud)* We'll break the door down ourselves if you don't open.

SECOND VOICE: *(Low)* Maybe she is not there.

FIRST VOICE: *(Low)* She is there. Where else would she be? She ran up the steps. There is only one door here. Where could she go? *(Loud)* Elizabeth Bam, I tell you for the last time, open the door. *(Pause.)* Break it down!

SECOND VOICE: You don't have a knife?

FIRST VOICE: No, do it with your shoulders.

SECOND VOICE: It won't give. Wait, I'll try this way.

E. B.: I shall not open the door till you tell me what you want to do with me.

FIRST VOICE: You know yourself what is ahead of you.

E. B.: No, I don't know; you want to kill me.

FIRST VOICE: You are due to receive severe punishment.

SECOND VOICE: No matter what, you will not escape us.

E. B.: Perhaps you will tell me what I am guilty of?

FIRST VOICE: You know it yourself.

E. B.:No, I don't know it.

FIRST VOICE: Permit us not to believe you.

SECOND VOICE: You are a criminal.

E. B.: Ho, ho, ho. If you kill me, you think you'll have a clear conscience?

FIRST VOICE: We'll do it in keeping with our conscience.

E. B.: In that case it is bad. Because you have no conscience.

SECOND VOICE: What do you mean, no conscience? Peter Nikolaevich, she says we have no conscience.

E. B.: You, Ivan Ivanovich, you have no conscience. You are simply a crook.

SECOND VOICE: Who is a crook? Me? Me? I am a crook?

FIRST VOICE: Wait, Ivan Ivanovich. Elizabeth Bam, I am ordering you.

SECOND VOICE: No, Peter Nikolaevich; I am a crook?

FIRST VOICE: Wait, don't get insulted. Elizabeth Bam, I order you.

SECOND VOICE: No, wait, Peter Nikolaevich; tell me, am I a crook?

FIRST VOICE: Forget it, will you?

SECOND VOICE: What, according to you I am a crook?

FIRST VOICE: Yes, a crook!

SECOND VOICE: Oh, so according to you I am a crook. That's what you have said.

FIRST VOICE: Go away! What a blockhead. And he has a responsible job. They said one word to you, and you are ready to climb a wall. After this what are you? Simply an idiot.

SECOND VOICE: You are a fake.

FIRST VOICE: Go away!

E. B.: Ivan Ivanovich is a crook.

SECOND VOICE: I won't forgive you for this.

FIRST VOICE: I'll throw you down the stairs right now.

IVAN: Try to throw me.

PETER: I will throw you. I will! I will!

(The door opens.)

E. B.: Your arms are too short for that.

PETER: My arms are too short?

IVAN: Yours are too short, yes. Say, aren't his arms too short?

E. B.: Yes, they are.

PETER: Elizabeth Bam, how dare you speak like that?

E. B.: Why?

PETER: Because you have no right to speak. You have committed a loathsome crime. It is not for you to tell me impertinent things. You are a criminal.

E. B.: Why?

PETER: What do you mean, why?

E. B.: Why am I a criminal?

PETER: Because you have no right to speak.

IVAN: No right to speak.

E. B.: Yes, I do have the right. You can verify it as much as you like.

PETER: Things will not go as far as that. I posted a guard at the door, and at the least push, Ivan will hiccup.

E. B.: Show me. Please, show me.

PETER: Well, look. I suggest you turn aside. One, two, three. *(He pushes the stand.)*

IVAN: *(Hiccups loudly.)*

E. B.: One more time, please. *(Pause. Ivan hiccups once more.)* How do you do it?

PETER: Very easily. Ivan Ivanovich, show us.

IVAN: With pleasure.

E. B.: This is just marvelous. *(Shouts)* Mother! Come here. Magicians are here. My mother will come right away. Meet Peter Nikolaevich, Ivan Ivanovich. Show us something.

IVAN: With pleasure.

PETER: Alley-oop. Right away, right away.

IVAN: There is nothing to lean against.

E. B.: Perhaps you would like a towel?

IVAN: What for?

E. B.: Only so. He, he, he, he.

IVAN: You have an extremely pleasant appearance.

E. B.: Yes, I guess so. Why?

IVAN: Y-y-y-y—because you are a forget-me-not. *(He hiccups loudly.)*

E. B.: I am a forget-me-not. That is true. And you are a tulip.

IVAN: What?

E. B.: A tulip.

IVAN: *(Puzzled)* Thank you very much.

E. B.: *(With a nasal twang)* Allow me to pick you.

FATHER: *(In a bass voice)* Elizabeth, don't act like a fool.

E. B.: *(To father)* Daddy, I'll stop right away. *(Twangingly)*
I-i-i-chu. Get down on all fours.

IVAN: If you allow me, Elizabeth Cockroachovna, I ought to go
home. My wife is waiting for me at home. She has a lot of
children, Elizabeth. Please forgive me for having been so
boring to you. Don't forget me. I am the kind of man that
everybody chases away. Why? What have I done? Have I
stolen anything? No. Elizabeth Eduardovna, I am an honest
person. I have a wife at home. My wife has many children.
They are good children. Each of them holds a matchbox in
his teeth. Forgive me. Elizabeth Mikhailovna, I'll go home.

> The morning blazed forth
> The water is red.

PETER:

> The seagull flies quickly over the lake, etcetera.
> We have arrived.

FATHER: Thank goodness. *(Leaves.)*

E. B.: Mother, you are not going out for a walk?

MOTHER: You want to?

E. B.: Terribly.

MOTHER: No, I won't go.

E. B.: Oh, come on, come on.

MOTHER: All right, let us go, let us go. *(They leave.)*
(The stage is empty.)

IVAN: Where, where, where are they?

PETER: *(Runs in.)* Elizabeth! Elizabeth! Elizabeth! Here, here, here.

IVAN: Over there, there, there.

PETER: Where are we, Ivan Ivanovich?

IVAN: Peter Nikolaevich, we are locked up.

PETER: How disgusting. Please don't touch me.

IVAN: Here is a pound. Five minus five is enough.

PETER: Where is Elizabeth Bam?

IVAN: What do you need her for?

PETER: To kill her.

IVAN: Oh, Elizabeth Bam is sitting on the little bench over there.

PETER: Let's run as fast as we can.

(Both run in place.)

> Hop, hop, our legs,
> Sunset is over the hills,
> Behind pink clouds.
> Whooo, whooo, the train,
> Tu-whoo, tu-whoo, the owl.

E. B.: Are you looking for me? *(She gets up and walks away.)*

PETER: Yes, Vanka, she is here.

IVAN: Where? Where?

PETER: Here under the little farm. *(A beggar enters.)*

IVAN: Pull her out.

PETER: She doesn't come out.

BEGGAR: *(To Elizabeth Bam)* Comrade, help me. *(Stammers)* Next time I'll be more experienced. I marked everything just now.

E. B.: *(To Beggar)* I don't have anything.

BEGGAR: Give me a penny.

E. B.: Ask that man over there. *(She points to Peter Nikolaevich.)*

PETER: *(Stammers)* Be careful what you are doing.

IVAN: *(Stammers)* I am digging out roots.

BEGGAR: Help, comrades.

PETER: *(To Beggar)* Here. Crawl in there.

IVAN: Lean on the stones with your hands.

PETER: He knows how.

E. B.: Sit down, too. Why, look!

IVAN: Thank you.

PETER: Let's sit down. *(He sits down.)*

E. B.: My husband isn't coming. Where did he get stuck?

PETER: He will come. *(He jumps up and runs around on the stage.)* Boohoo!

IVAN: Ho, ho, ho. *(Runs after Peter.)* Where is safe?

E. B.: Here, behind this line.

PETER: *(Hits Ivan.)* You are it.

E. B.: Ivan Ivanovich, let us run here.

IVAN: Ho, ho, ho, I have no legs.

PETER: On all fours.

FATHER: *(To the audience)* It has been written about her . . .

E. B.: Who is it?

IVAN: Me—ha, ha, ha—with my pants on.

PETER AND E. B.: Ho, ho, ho.

FATHER: Copernicus was a very great scholar.

IVAN: *(Falls on the floor.)* I have hair on my head.

PETER AND E. B.: Ho, ho, ho, ho.

IVAN: I am lying on the floor.

PETER: Ho, ho, ho, ho.

E. B.: Oh, I can't help laughing.

FATHER: When you buy a fowl, see if it has teeth. If it has teeth, it is not a fowl.

PETER: *(Raises his hand.)* Please listen to me. I want to prove to you that all misfortune begins unexpectedly. When I was still a very young man, I lived in a small house with a creaking door. I lived alone in that house. Except for me, there were only mice and cockroaches. Cockroaches everywhere. When night fell, I locked the door and put out the lamp. I slept fearing nothing.

A VOICE BEHIND THE STAGE: Nothing.

MOTHER: Nothing.

PIPE BEHIND THE STAGE: Ee, eee.

IVAN: Nothing.

PIANO: Eeeeee.

PETER: Nothing. *(Pause.)* I had nothing to be afraid of. Really. Robbers might come and search the house. What would they find? Nothing.

PIPE BEHIND THE STAGE: Eeee, eeee. *(Pause.)*

PETER: And who else might come at night? Nobody. Right?

VOICE BEHIND THE STAGE: Nobody.

PETER: Right? But once I wake up and I see the door is open, and some woman is standing in the doorway. I stare right at her. She is standing there. There was enough light. It must have been getting close to dawn. In any case I saw her face well. That is who it was. *(He points at Elizabeth Bam.)* At that time she looked like . . .

ALL: Like me.

IVAN: I speak so that I will continue to exist.

E. B.: What are you saying?

IVAN: I speak so that I will continue to exist. Then I think it is too late. She hears me. I ask her what she had done. She says she had a fight with him with backswords. It was an honest fight, but she is not to be blamed for killing him. Think. Why did you kill Peter Nikolaevich?

E. B.: Hurrah, I did not kill anybody.

Ivan: To take a human being and knife him. That is so perfidious. Hurrah, you did it. Why did you?

E. B.: *(Walks to the side.)* Whoooooooooooooo.

Ivan: She-wolf!

E. B.: *(Trembles.)* Whooooooo—black prunes.

Ivan: Great-grandmother.

E. B.: Jubilation!

Ivan: She is destroyed forever.

E. B.: Black horse, and on the horse a soldier.

Ivan: *(Lights a match.)* Dear, darling Elizabeth.

E. B.: My shoulders are like the rising sun. *(She climbs onto a chair.)*

Ivan: *(Squats down.)* My legs are like cucumbers. *(Lies down on the floor.)* No, no, nothing.

E. B.: *(Raises her arms.)* Ku-ni-na-ga ni-li-va-ni-ba-oo-oo.

Ivan: *(Lying on the floor)* Fowl, fowl.

> Murka the cat
> Lapped up the milk
> Jumped on the pillow
> Jumped on the stove
> > Jump, jump,
> > Leap, leap.

E. B.: *(Shouts)* Two gates, shirt, twine.

Ivan: *(Raising himself halfway up)* Two carpenters have come and ask, "What is the matter?"

E. B.: Cutlets, Barbara Semyonovna.

IVAN: *(Shouts, clenching his teeth)* Dancer on the ro-o-o-ope.

E. B.: *(Jumps onto a chair.)* I am all shiny. *(Runs far into the room.)* We don't know how many cubic feet there are in this room. *(Runs to the other end of the stage.)* It's all in the family; we'll work it out.

IVAN: *(Jumps onto a chair.)* All best wishes to the Pennsylvania shepherd, and she . . .

E. B.: *(Jumps onto a second chair.)* Ivan Ivaaa———.

FATHER: *(Shows a little box.)* The box is made of wooooo———.

IVAN: *(From the chair)* So far . . .

FATHER: Take it and looook.

MOTHER: Looooo———.

E. B.: I found mushrooms.

IVAN: Let's go to the lake.

FATHER: A-ooooooo.

E. B.: A-ooooooo.

IVAN: Yesterday I met Kolka.

MOTHER: You don't say.

IVAN: Yes, yes. I met him, met him. I see him coming and carrying apples. "You bought them?" say I. "Yes, I bought them," says he. Then he took them and went away.

FATHER: You don't say.

IVAN: Well, yes, I asked him, "Did you buy them or steal them?" "Bought them"—and he went away.

MOTHER: Where did he go away to?

IVAN: I don't know. He only said, "Me"— he says—"I bought the apples; I did not steal them"—and he went away.

FATHER: After this not altogether gracious welcome, the sister conducted her to a more open spot, where gold tables and armchairs were placed, and fifteen young beauties merrily prattled among themselves, sitting on whatever was around. All these maidens badly needed a hot iron, and all were distinguished by a strange manner of rolling their eyes without ceasing to chatter for one moment.

IVAN: Friends, we are all gathered here. Hurrah!

E. B.: Hurrah!

MOTHER AND FATHER: Hurrah!

IVAN: *(Trembling and lighting a match)* I want to tell you that since the time I was born thirty-eight years have passed.

FATHER AND MOTHER: Hurrah!

IVAN: Comrades. I have a house. My wife is sitting at home. She has many children. I have counted them: ten children.

MOTHER: *(Marking time)* Darya, Marya, Fyodor, Pelegeya, Nina, and four others.

FATHER: All boys?

E. B.: *(Runs around the stage.)* She tore herself away and ran. Tore herself away and ran.

MOTHER: *(Runs behind her.)* Do you eat bread?

E. B.: Do you eat soup?

FATHER: Do you eat meat?

MOTHER: Do you eat flour?

IVAN: Do you eat turnips? *(He runs.)*

E. B.: Do you eat mutton?

FATHER: Do you eat cutlets?

MOTHER: Ouch, my legs are tired.

IVAN: Ouch, my arms are tired.

E. B.: Ouch, the scissors are tired.

FATHER: Ouch, the springs are tired.

MOTHER: The door to the balcony is open.

IVAN: I should like to jump up to the fourth floor.

E. B.: Tore off and ran, tore off and ran.

FATHER: Help! My right hand and nose are the same as my left hand and ear.

CHORUS: *(To a melody like the motif of the overture)*

> So long, so long.
> Up above the pine tree speaks
> And round about darkness
> On the pine the bed speaks
> And in the bed lies the husband
> So long, so long.
> Somehow once we ran up
> Into an endless house
> And a young old man looks through the window
> Up above through his glasses
> So long, so long.
> The gate opened
> There appeared . . .

(Overture)

IVAN: You are broken. Your chair is broken.

VIOLIN:

> Na na ni na
> Na na ni na.

IVAN:

> Rise like Berlin.
>   Put on a pelerine.

VIOLIN:

> Na na ni na
> Na na ni na.

IVAN:

> Eight minutes
>> Will pass unnoticed.

VIOLIN:

> Na na ni na na.
> Na na ni.

IVAN: You have been given the bill.

> Wake up, heavies,
> A squad or platoon
> To pull the machine gun.

DRUM:

| |

    | | |

       | | | |

IVAN:

> Shreds flew
> One week after another.

SIREN AND DRUM:

> Viaa boom boom
> Viaa boom boom.

IVAN:

> The bride didn't notice
> The captain's fool who was free of charge.

SIREN: Whooeey, whooeey.

IVAN:

> Help me, now help me!
> Salad and water are above me.

VIOLIN:

> Pa pa pi pa
> Pa pa pi pa.

IVAN: Say, Peter Nikolaevich, you've been up there on that mountain?

PETER: I've just come from there. It's beautiful over there. Flowers grow there. Trees. A little wooden cottage stands there.

> In the little cottage there is a little fire
> Black bugs fly around the fire
> Moths knock against the windows.
> From time to time the rascals flit and fly around in a chain
> Under the roof and flutter the air
> And send into the emptiness before them
> Invisible chirping answers.
> Conspiracy hums in all melodies.

IVAN:

> And in this little house which is made of wood,
> Which is called a cottage,
> In which a little fire glows and stirs about,
> Who lives in this little house?

PETER:

> Nobody lives in it,
> And nobody opens the door
> Only the mice rub the flour in it with the palms of their feet,
> Only the lamp shines like rosemary
> And all day the cockroach sits on the stove like a hermit.

IVAN: And who lights the lamp?

PETER: Nobody; it burns all by itself.

IVAN: But that never happens.

PETER:

> Empty stupid words.
> There is an endless movement,
> The breathing of light elements.
> The planets' course, the earth's turning,
> The day's and night's crazy alternation,
> The wrath and strength of sleeping animals
> And the overcoming by man
> Of the laws of the light and the wave.

IVAN: *(Lighting a match)*

> Now I have understood, understood, understood.
> I thank you and I join you sitting down.
> As always, I am interested.
> What time is it? tell me.

PETER:

> Four o'clock. Oh, it is dinner time.
> Ivan Ivanovich, tomorrow night
> Elizabeth Bam will die.

FATHER: *(Enters.)*

> Which Elizabeth Bam?
> The one who is my daughter?
> Whom tomorrow night you want to kill
> And string up on a pine tree?
> Who is good-looking?
> So that the animals all around
> And the whole country will know it.
> And I order you
> By the might of my arm
> To forget Elizabeth Bam
> Despite the laws.

PETER:

> Just try to forbid it,
> I'll trample you in a moment
> Then with red lashes
> I'll break your bones
> I'll cut them up, blow them up, and
> Float them downwind like flames.

IVAN:

> Everything around is known to him
> He is my commander and my friend
> With one motion of the wing
> He moves the oceans
> With one swing of the axe
> He fells forests and mountains
> With one movement
> He escapes capture.

FATHER:

> Let us fight, wizard,
> You with a word, I with my arm
> A minute will pass, an hour
> Then another.
> You will perish, I will perish.
> Everything will be quiet.
> But let my daughter Elizabeth Bam rejoice.

IVAN:

> The fight of two knights.
> Texts of Emmanuel Kriedeiteirik.
> Music by the Netherlandish shepherd Veliopag.
> Choreography by an unknown traveler.
> The beginning will be marked by a bell.

VOICES FROM VARIOUS PARTS OF THE AUDITORIUM: Fight of two
   knights [*etc.*]
BELL: Boom, boom, boom.
PETER:

    Kurybyr doramur
    Dyndiri
      Skalatyr pakaradagu
            Da ky chiri, kiri kiri
            Andudila khabakula
               Kheel
    Khangu ana kudy
      Para by na lyytena
          Kheeeeeel
      Chapu, agapaii
      Chapataii mar
      Labalochina
         Kheel. (*Raises his arm.*)

FATHER:

    Let the winged parrot
    Fly to the sun
    Let the golden wide day darken.
    Let the hoof's sounding and pounding
    Break through the forests
    And the heavy chest
    Fall off the wheel.
    The knight sitting at table
      Reaching for the sword
    Will lift the cup and
    Then shout above the cup:
      I lift up this cup

To raptured lips
And drink to the best one of all
   Elizabeth Bam
Whose fresh white hands
   Caressed my coat.
Elizabeth Bam
   Live a hundred thousand years.

PETER:

   Well, let's start.
      Please follow attentively the flitting
   Of our swords
   Where each directs its edge
      And where each takes direction.

IVAN:

   I cut to the side, I cut to the right,
   Let everyone save himself who can
      Where the grove rustles,
      Parks grow around.

PETER:

   Look less to the sides
   Pay more attention to the motion
      Of iron centers and the thickening of fatal forces.

FATHER:

   Glory to the iron carborundum,
      It reinforces pavements,
   And shines electrically,
   Tortures the enemy to death.
   Glory to iron! A song to battle!
   It excites the outlaw
   Makes a boy a youth

Tortures the enemy to death,
Oh sing to battle!
　　Glory to feathers!
They fly around in the air
Fill eyes of the faithless
　　Torture the enemy to death.
Oh glory to feathers! Wisdom to the stone.
The stone lies under the serious pine
And the water runs under it,
　　To meet the dead enemy.

PETER:

I fell on the earth defeated.
Good-by, Elizabeth Bam
Come to my house on the mountain,
　　And stay there.
Mice will run around on you
And will leave their droppings on your arms
And after them, the hermit cockroach.
　　You hear the bell resound
　　On the roof, dingdong.
　　Excuse me and forgive,
　　Elizabeth Bam.

IVAN: The fight of the two knights is finished.

E. B.: *(Enters.)* Oh, daddy, you are here. I am very glad. I was just in the co-op, bought candy. I wanted some cake for tea.

FATHER: *(Opens the door.)* Phoo, I got tired.

E. B.: What were you doing?

FATHER: I was chopping wood and got terribly tired.

E. B.: Ivan Ivanovich, run down to the grocery store and get us a bottle of beer and some peas.

IVAN: Oh, get some peas and run to the beer and bring the store.

E. B.: Not bring the store, but bring a bottle of beer, and go to some peas.

IVAN: Right away; I'll hide my hat in the store and will wear the beer on my head.

E. B.: Oh, no, no, but hurry; father got tired chopping wood.

FATHER: Women don't understand things; they have little sense.

MOTHER: *(Enters.)* Comrades. That villainess over there has bumped off my son.

HEADS: Who, who?

MOTHER: That one over there, with those lips like that.

E. B.: Mother, mother, what are you saying?

MOTHER: Only because of you his life all came to nothing.

E. B.: Tell me, who are you talking about?

MOTHER: *(With a stony face)* About him, him, him.

E. B.: She has lost her mind.

MOTHER: I am a cuttlefish.

E. B.: Right now they're going to come. What have I done?

MOTHER: Three times 27 makes 81.

E. B.: They'll certainly come in so that they can catch me and wipe me off the face of the earth. I must run, run. But where? This door leads to the stairs, and on the stairs I would run into them. Out the window? *(She looks out the window.)* Oh, oh, oh, I can't jump. It is very high. But what can I do? Whose steps? It is them. I'll lock the door and I won't open. Let them knock as much as they want.

(Knocking on the door.)

FIRST VOICE: Elizabeth Bam, in the name of the law I order you to open the door.

(Silence.)

FIRST VOICE: I order you to open the door. *(Silence.)*

SECOND VOICE: *(Quietly)* Let's break down the door.

FIRST VOICE: Elizabeth Bam, open up; otherwise we'll break down the door.

E. B.: What do you want to do with me?

FIRST VOICE: You will be severely punished.

E. B.: Why? Why don't you want to tell me what I have done?

FIRST VOICE: You are accused of having murdered Peter Nikolaevich.

SECOND VOICE: And you will answer for it.

E. B.: But I have not killed anybody.

FIRST VOICE: The court will decide that.

E. B.: I am in your power.

PETER: In the name of the law, you are arrested.

IVAN: *(Lights a match.)* Come with us!

THE END

STORIES FOR CHILDREN

by Daniil Kharms

A Children's Story

"Here," Vanya said, and put a notebook on the table, "let's
write a story."

"Let's," Lenochka said, and sat down in a chair.

Vanya took a pencil and wrote: "Once upon a time there
lived a king."

Then Vanya started to think and to look up at the ceiling.
Lenochka looked in the notebook and read what Vanya had
written.

"There already is a story like that," Lenochka said.

"How do you know?" Vanya asked.

"I know because I read it," Lenochka said.

"How does the story go?" Vanya asked.

"A king was drinking tea with apples in it, and something
stuck in his throat, and the queen pounded him on the back so
the piece of apple would come out, and the king thought the
queen was starting a fight, so he hit her over the head with a
glass. The queen got mad and hit the king with a plate. The
king hit the queen with a dish. The queen hit the king with a
chair. The king jumped up and hit the queen with a table. The
queen turned a cupboard over on the king. But the king
crawled out from under the cupboard and smashed the queen
with his crown. Then the queen caught the king by his hair
and threw him out the window. But the king crawled back
into the room through another window, grabbed the queen,

and shoved her into the stove. But the queen crawled up through the chimney onto the roof and then climbed down the lightning conductor and into the garden and came back into the room through the window. The king was making a fire in the stove to burn up the queen. The queen sneaked up behind him and gave him a push. The king fell into the stove and burned up. That's the end of the story," Lenochka said.

"That's a very stupid story," Vanya said. "I wanted to write a completely different one."

"So go ahead and write it," Lenochka said.

Vanya took the pencil and wrote: "Once upon a time there lived a bandit."

"Wait a minute!" Lenochka shouted. "There already is a fairy tale like that."

"I didn't know that," Vanya said.

"Why, you know," Lenochka said, "a bandit was trying to run away from a guardsman and jumped on a horse, but jumped too hard and fell off the other side and dropped down on the ground. The bandit cursed and again jumped on the horse, but again he didn't figure his jump right, and fell over on the other side and fell on the ground. The bandit got up, shook his fist, jumped on the horse, and again jumped too far and fell down on the ground. At that point the bandit pulled a pistol from his belt, shot into the air, and again jumped on the horse, but with such force that he flew over it and hit the ground. Then the bandit tore his cap off his head, stomped on it with his feet, and again jumped up on the horse, and again jumped too far, fell on the ground, and broke his leg. The horse walked away a little. The bandit limped up to the horse and hit it on the head with his fist. The horse ran away. Guardsmen rode up, arrested the bandit, and took him to jail."

"I'm not going to write about a bandit," Vanya said.

"What are you going to write about?" Lenochka asked.

"I'm going to write a story about a blacksmith," Vanya said.

Vanya wrote: "Once up on a time there lived a blacksmith."

"There is a story like that already!" Lenochka shouted.

"Oh," said Vanya, and put his pencil down.

"Of course," Lenochka said. "Once upon a time there was a blacksmith. Once he was making a horseshoe, and he swung his hammer so hard that the hammer head flew off the handle, flew out the window, killed four pigeons, hit a fire tower, flew off to the side, broke a window in the fire chief's house, flew over the table where the fire chief and his wife were sitting, broke the wall in the fire chief's house, and flew out onto the street. There it knocked over a lamppost, knocked an ice-cream man off his feet, and hit Karl Ivanovich Shusterling on the head. He had taken his hat off for a moment to cool off the back of his head. After hitting the head of Karl Ivanovich Shusterling, the hammer head flew backward, again knocked the ice-cream man off his feet, knocked two fighting cats off the roof, knocked over a cow, killed four sparrows, again flew into the blacksmith shop, and flew back onto the handle which the smith was still holding in his right hand. All this happened so quickly that the smith didn't notice anything and kept on making a horseshoe."

"So that means a story has already been written about a smith; so I'll write a story about myself," Vanya said, and wrote: "Once upon a time there was a boy whose name was Vanya."

"There already is a story like that," Lenochka said. "Once upon a time there was a boy whose name was Vanya, and once he went up to . . ."

"Wait a minute," Vanya said; "I wanted to write a story about myself."

"A story has already been written about you," Lenochka said.

"That's impossible," Vanya said.

"I tell you it's already been written," Lenochka said.

"Where has it been written?" Vanya asked, astonished.

"Buy Number 7 of the magazine *Chizh,* and you can read the story about yourself," Lenochka said.

Vanya bought *Chizh,* Number 7, and read in it the same story you have just finished reading.

How Kolka Pankin Flew to Brazil and Petka Ershov Wouldn't Believe Anything

1

Kolka Pankin decided to go someplace very far away.

"I'm going to Brazil," he told Petka Ershov.

"Where is Brazil?" Petka asked.

"Brazil is in South America," Kolka said. "It's very hot there. People raise monkeys and parrots there. Palm trees grow there; hummingbirds fly around; there are wild animals and savage tribes."

"Indians?" asked Petka.

"Sort of like Indians," Kolka said.

"How does one get there?" Petka asked.

"By airplane or by boat," Kolka said.

"How are you going to go?" Petka asked.

"I'll fly in an airplane," Kolka said.

"Where are you going to get an airplane?" Petka asked.

"I'll go to the airport, ask for one, and they'll let me have it," Kolka said.

"And who will give it to you?" Petka asked.

"I know all of them there," Kolka said.

"Who are all the people you know there?" Petka asked.

"All sorts of people," Kolka said.

"You don't know anybody there," Petka said.

"I do," Kolka said.

"No, you don't," Petka said.

"I do."

"No, you don't."

"I do."

"No, you don't."

Kolka Pankin and Petka Ershov decided to go to the airport next morning.

2

Kolka Pankin and Petka Ershov went early next morning. It was a long way to the airport, but the weather was nice. They didn't have the streetcar fare, so Kolka and Petka went on foot.

"I'll certainly go to Brazil," Kolka said.

"Will you send me a letter?" Petka asked.

"I will," Kolka said, "and when I come back, I'll bring you a monkey."

"Will you bring me a bird?" Petka asked.

"I'll bring you a bird, too," Kolka said, "any kind of bird you want. A hummingbird or a parrot?"

"Which is better?" Petka asked.

"The parrot is better; it can talk," Kolka said.

"Can it sing?" Petka asked.

"It can sing, too," Kolka said.

"Can it read music?" Petka asked.

"It can't read music. But you can sing anything you want, and the parrot will repeat it," Kolka said.

"And will you really bring me a parrot?" Petka asked.

"I really will," Kolka said.

"And what if you don't?" Petka asked.

"I said I will bring it, so that means I'll bring it," Kolka said.

"You won't bring it," Petka said.

"I will," Kolka said.

"You won't," Petka said.

"I will," Kolka said.

"You won't."

"I will."

"You won't."

"I will."

"You won't."

But at that point Kolka Pankin and Petka Ershov arrived at the airport.

3

The airport was very interesting. The airplanes rode around on the ground one after the other, and then, one, two, three, they were up in the air, first low down and then higher and then still higher, and then they circled around and flew away altogether. Eight more airplanes were standing on the ground also ready to start and fly away. Kolka Pankin picked out one of them, pointed it out to Petka Ershov, and said, "This is the one I'll fly to Brazil in."

Petka took his cap off and scratched his head. He put his cap back on again and asked, "They're going to let you have that airplane?"

"They will," Kolka said; "I know a pilot here."

"You know him? What's his name?" Petka asked.

"His name is simply Pavel Ivanovich," Kolka said.

"Pavel Ivanovich?" Petka asked, to make sure.

"Yes, that's right," Kolka said.

"You will ask him for a plane?" Petka asked.

"Of course. Let's go together; you can listen," Kolka said.

"And what if he won't let you have the plane?" Petka asked.

"What do you mean, won't let me have the plane? I'll ask him and he'll let me have it," Kolka said.

"And what if you don't ask him?" Petka asked.

"I will," Kolka said.

"You'll get scared," Petka said.

"No, I won't get scared," Kolka said.

"A little bit," Petka said.

"Not even a little bit," Kolka said.

"A little bit," Petka said.

"No, not a little bit," Kolka said.

"A little bit."

"Not a little bit."

"A little bit."

"Not a little bit."

Kolka Pankin and Petka Ershov ran over to the pilot.

4

The pilot was standing near a plane and washing little screws of some kind in gasoline in a pan. He was dressed all in leather, and beside him, on the ground, lay leather gloves and a leather helmet.

Kolka Pankin and Petka Ershov went up to him.

The pilot picked screws out of the gasoline, put them on the edge of the plane, and put different screws into the gasoline and started washing them.

Kolka looked and looked, and then he said: "Hi, Pavel Ivanovich."

The pilot looked first at Kolka, then at Petka, and then

turned away again. Kolka stood there, and stood there, and said again: "Hi, Pavel Ivanovich."

The pilot then looked first at Petka and then at Kolka and then said, rubbing one foot with the other foot: "My name isn't Pavel Ivanovich; my name is Constantine Constantinovich. I don't know any Pavel Ivanovich."

Petka burst out laughing, Kolka hit Petka, Petka put on a serious expression, and Kolka told the pilot: "Constantine Constantinovich, Petka Ershov and me, we decided we would fly to Brazil. Won't you lend us your airplane?"

The pilot started to laugh: "Ho, ho, ho, ho, ho, ho. You what? Seriously—you decided you would fly to Brazil?"

"Yes," Kolka said.

"Will you fly us?" Petka asked.

"What did you think?" the pilot shouted. "You thought I would give you a plane? No, kids. But if you paid me, I would take you to Brazil. How much will you give me?"

Kolka poked around in his pockets but found nothing.

"We don't have any money," he said to the pilot; "maybe you would take us for free?"

"No, I won't take you for free," the pilot said, and turned around and started fixing something or other in the plane.

Kolka waved one arm and yelled: "Constantine Constantinovich! Do you want a jackknife? A very good one, with three blades. Two are broken, but one is whole, and it's very sharp. Once I threw it at a door, and it went all the way through."

"When was that?" Petka asked.

"What business is it of yours? It was last winter." Kolka became angry.

"What door was it the knife went all the way through?" Petka asked.

"The door to the storeroom," Kolka said.

"It doesn't have any hole in it," Petka said.

"They must have put in a new door," Kolka said.

"No, they didn't; it's the old door," Petka said.

"No, it's a new one," Kolka said.

"Give me that knife," Petka said; "it's my knife; I only lent it to you to cut the clothesline, and you kept it."

"What do you mean, your knife? It's my knife," Kolka said.

"No, it's my knife," said Petka.

"No, mine," said Kolka.

"No, mine," said Petka.

"No, mine."

"No, mine."

"All right, kids, darn it," the pilot said. "Jump in, kids; get in the plane; we'll fly to Brazil."

5

Kolka Pankin and Petka Ershov flew to Brazil in an airplane. It was really interesting.

The pilot sat in the front seat; you could only see his helmet. Everything was very nice; the motor made a lot of noise; it was hard to talk. And when you looked down from the plane to the earth, it was so huge you caught your breath. Everything down on the ground was so tiny—teeny-weeny—and turned the wrong way around.

"Pet-ka!" Kolka shouted. "Look at that icky town."

"What?" Petka shouted.

"The town!" Kolka shouted.

"Can't hear you," Petka shouted.

"What?" Kolka shouted.

"How soon do we get to Brazil?" Petka shouted.

"Which Brazil?" Kolka shouted.

"My cap flew away!" Petka shouted.

"How many?" Kolka shouted.

"Yesterday," Petka shouted.

"North America," Kolka shouted.

"Navidarieedee!" Petka shouted.

"What?" Kolka shouted.

Suddenly their ears popped, and the plane started to go down.

6

The plane bounced up and down on the bumps in the field and stopped.

"Here we are," the pilot said.

Kolka Pankin and Petka Ershov looked around.

"Petka," Kolka said, "see what Brazil looks like."

"This is Brazil?" Petka asked.

"Can't you see for yourself, idiot?" Kolka said.

"Who are those people running over there?" Petka asked.

"Where? Oh, I see," Kolka said. "Those are the natives, the savages."

"You see, they wear a white headdress. They make the headdress out of grass and straw."

"What for?" Petka asked.

"Just because," Kolka said.

"But look, I think it's their hair," Petka said.

"And I tell you it's feathers," Kolka said.

"No, hair," Petka said.

"No, feathers," Kolka said.

"No, hair."

"No, feathers."

"No, hair."

"Well, get out of the plane," the pilot said; "I've got to fly back."

7

Kolka Pankin and Petka Ershov got out of the plane and went to meet the natives. The natives turned out to be small, dirty, and blond. When they saw Kolka and Petka, the natives stood still. Kolka stepped forward, raised his right arm, and said, "Oakh!" in the Indian language.

The natives opened their mouths and stood there in silence.

"Gapakook!" Kolka said to them in the Indian language.

"What is it you're saying to them?" Petka asked.

"I am talking with them in Indian," Kolka said.

"Where did you learn Indian?" Petka asked.

"I had a kind of book, and I learned it from the book," Kolka said.

"Oh, come on, you're lying," Petka said.

"Shut up!" Kolka said. "Inam kos!" he told the natives in Indian.

The natives started to laugh.

"Kerek eri yale," the natives said.

"Ara toki," Kolka said.

"Meeta?" the native asked.

"That's enough; let's get a move on," Petka said.

"Peelgedrau!" Kolka shouted.

"Perkilya!" the natives shouted.

"Koolmegooynky," Kolka shouted.

"Perkilya, perkilya," the natives shouted.

"Let's run," Petka shouted, "They want to fight."

But it was too late. The natives jumped Kolka and started to beat him.

"Help!" Kolka shouted.

"Perkilya!" the natives shouted.

"Moo," the cow mooed.

8

After they had beaten up Kolka, the natives picked up dirt and threw it in the air, and ran away. Kolka stood there, looking a mess.

"Pe-pet-ka," he stammered, "I really beat up those natives. I hit one of them like this and another like that."

"I thought it was they who beat you up," Petka said.

"Oh, come on," Kolka said. "I went after them like this: one-two, one-two, one-two."

"Moo," something said right near Kolka's ear.

"Ouch!" Kolka yelped, and ran away.

"Kolka, Kolka," Petka shouted.

But Kolka ran away without looking back.

> They ran and they ran,
> They ran and they ran,
> They ran and they ran,
> And Kolka only stopped when he reached the woods.

"Oop," he said, breathing deeply.

Petka was so out of breath he couldn't say anything.

"A bison," Kolka said when he managed to catch his breath.

"What?" Petka asked.

"Didn't you see the bison?" Kolka asked.

"Where?" Petka asked.

"Why, over there. It was rushing right at us," Kolka said.

"Wasn't it a cow?" Petka asked.

"Oh, come, what kind of cow? In Brazil they don't have any cows," Kolka said.

"Do bison run around with bells on their necks?" Petka asked.

"They do," Kolka said.

"Where do the bells come from?" Petka asked.

"From the Indians. The Indians always capture a bison, tie a bell to his neck, and let him go again."

"What for?" Petka said.

"Just because," Kolka said.

"Its not true; bison don't go around with bells, and it was a cow," Petka said.

"No, a bison," said Kolka.

"No, a cow," said Petka.

"No, a bison."

"No, a cow."

"No, a bison."

"And where are the parrots?" asked Petka.

9

Kolka Pankin was taken aback.

"What parrots?" he asked Petka Ershov.

"You promised me you would catch a parrot as soon as we got to Brazil. If this is Brazil, then there must be parrots," Petka said.

"I don't see any parrots, but there are hummingbirds over there," Kolka said.

"Over there on the pine tree?" Petka asked.

"That's not a pine tree but a palm tree," Kolka said, offended.

"Palm trees look different in pictures," Petka said.

"In pictures they look different, but in Brazil they look like this," Kolka said angrily. "You'd do better to look and see what kind of hummingbirds there are."

"They look like our sparrows," Petka said.

"They look like sparrows," Kolka agreed, "but they're smaller."

"No, bigger," Petka said.

"No, smaller," Kolka said.

"No. bigger," Petka said.

"No, smaller," Kolka said.

"No, bigger."

"No, smaller."

"No, bigger."

"No, smaller."

Suddenly, Kolka and Petka heard a loud noise behind them.

10

Kolka Pankin and Petka Ershov turned around.

Some kind of monster was rushing straight at them.

"What's that?" Kolka said, frightened.

"That's a car," Petka said.

"It can't be," Kolka said. "How would a car get to Brazil?"

"I don't know," Petka said, "but that's a car."

"Can't be," Kolka said.

"And I tell you, it's a car," Petka said.

"Can't be," Kolka said.

"It can."

"No, it can't."

"Now do you see it's a car?" Petka asked.

"I see it, but it's very strange," Kolka said.

In the meantime the car had driven up very close.

"Hey kids," the man in the car shouted. "Is the way to Leningrad right or left?"

"What Leningrad?" Kolka asked.

"What do you mean, what Leningrad? Which way is it to town?" the driver asked.

"We don't know," Petka said, and then, suddenly, he screamed.

"Mister," he screamed, "please give us a ride to town."

"Do you live in town?" the driver asked.

"Yes," Petka screamed, "on Mokhovaya Street."

"How did you ever get out here?" the driver asked, surprised.

"It was Kolka," Petka screamed; "he promised to take us to Brazil, and he got us here."

"To Brusilovo, Brusilovo. Wait a minute; Brusilovo is further off, over somewhere around Chernigov," the driver said.

"Chiligov. Chilean republic. Chile. That is further south; that's where Argentina is. Chile is on the shore of the Pacific Ocean," Kolka said.

"Mister," Petka sobbed, "give us a ride home."

"All right, all right," the driver said. "Get in; the car's empty anyway. But Brusilovo is over by Chernigov."

So Kolka Pankin and Petka Ershov rode home in the car.

11

At first Kolka Pankin and Petka Ershov rode in silence. Then Kolka looked at Petka and said, "Petka"—Kolka said—"did you see the condor?"

"No," Petka said. "What's that?"

"It's a bird," Kolka said.

"A big one?" Petka asked.

"A very big one," Kolka said.

"Bigger than a crow?" Petka asked.

"Why, it's the biggest bird there is," Kolka said.

"I didn't see it," Petka said.

"I did see it. It sat on the palm tree," Kolka said.

"What palm tree?" Petka asked.

"On the palm tree the hummingbird was sitting on," Kolka said.

"That wasn't a palm tree but a pine tree," Petka said.

"No, a palm tree," Kolka said.

"No, a pine tree," Petka said. "Palms grow only in Brazil, and they don't grow here."

"We were in Brazil," Kolka said.

"No, we were not," Petka said.

"Yes, we were," Kolka said.

"We were not," Petka shouted.

"We were, were, were, were," Kolka shouted.

"There's Leningrad now," the driver said, and pointed at the chimneys and roofs rising up against the sky.

THE END

CHRISTMAS AT THE IVANOVS'

by Alexander Vvedensky

CAST OF CHARACTERS [1]

Petya Perov, 1-year-old boy
Nina Serova, 8-year-old girl
Varya Petrova, 17-year-old girl
Volodya Komarov, 25-year-old boy   the children
Sonia Ostrova, 32-year-old girl
Misha Pestrov, 76-year-old boy
Dunya Shustrova, 82-year-old girl
Mother Puzyrov
Father Puzyrov
Vera, a dog
Gravedigger
Chambermaids, cooks, soldiers, teachers of Latin and Greek

The action takes place in the 1890's.

---

[1] The cast of characters is that given in the manuscript of Vvedensky's play. In actual fact the cast also includes nurses, Fyodor, a clerk, policemen, woodcutters, a medical attendant, a doctor, patients, judges, court employees, a secretary, a giraffe, a wolf, a lion, and a piglet.—Ed.

Act I

Scene i

(A painted bathtub. It is Christmas Eve, so the children are having a bath. There is also a chest of drawers. To the right of the door, cooks are slaughtering chickens and slaughtering suckling pigs. Nurses, nurses, nurses are washing the children. All the children are sitting in one big bathtub, but Petya Perov, the 1-year-old boy, is having his bath in a pan which is directly in front of the door. A clock hangs on the wall to the left of the door. It shows 9:00 P.M.)

PETYA PEROV, 1-year-old boy: Will there be Christmas? Yes, there will be. And then suddenly there will not be. Suddenly I shall die.

NURSE: *(Gloomy as a skunk)* Wash yourself, Petya Perov. Soap your ears and neck. You don't know how to talk yet.

PETYA PEROV, 1-year-old boy: I know how to talk in my thoughts. I know how to cry. I know how to laugh. What do you want?

VARYA PETROVA, 17-year-old girl: Volodya, scrub my back. God knows there is moss growing on it. What do you think?

VOLODYA KOMAROV, 25-year-old boy: I think nothing. I burned my stomach.

MISHA PESTROV, 76-year-old boy: Now you will have a spot. Which I know nothing will be able to remove, ever.

SONIA OSTROVA, 32-year-old girl: You, Misha, you always say

the wrong things. You would do better to look and see how big my breasts have become.

DUNYA SHUSTROVA, 82-year-old girl: Again you are bragging. You were bragging about your buttocks, and now about your breasts. You ought to fear God.

SONIA OSTROVA, 32-year-old girl: (*Hangs her head like a grown-up* Ukrainian.) I am mad at you. You fool, you idiot, you whore!

NURSE: (*Waving an axe as though it were a small hatchet*) Sonia, if you use bad language, I'll tell your father and mother, and I'll kill you with the axe.

PETYA PEROV, 1-year-old boy: And you'll feel, for a brief moment, how your skin splits open and how the blood spurts out. And what you'll feel after that is unknown.

NINA SEROVA, 8-year-old girl: Sonechka, that nurse is either a lunatic or a criminal. She is capable of doing anything. Why did they ever hire her?

MISHA PESTROV, 76-year-old boy: Children, stop fighting. At this rate you won't even live to see Christmas. And our parents have bought candles, candy, and matches to light the candles with.

SONIA OSTROVA, 32-year-old girl: I don't need candles. I have a finger.

VARYA PETROVA, 17-year-old girl: Sonia, don't keep on like that. Don't keep on. Better wash yourself.

VOLODYA KOMAROV, 25-year-old boy: Girls must wash more often than boys, or they become repulsive. That's what I think.

MISHA PESTROV, 76-year-old boy: Oh, you say such nasty things. Tomorrow is Christmas, and we will be all merry.

PETYA PEROV, 1-year-old boy: Only I shall sit on everybody's lap in turn, on every guest's lap, looking serious and stupid, as if I understood nothing. I and invisible God.

SONIA OSTROVA, 32-year-old girl: And when I come into the room, when they light the candles on the Christmas tree, I'll lift up my skirt and show everything to everybody.

NURSE: (*Getting angry*) No, you won't show anything. You have nothing to show. You are still little.

SONIA OSTROVA, 32-year-old girl: No, I'll show everything. But I do still have a little one; you are right about that. That's better. Not like yours.

NURSE: (*Picks up the axe and chops off her head.*) You deserved this death.

CHILDREN: (*Scream*) Murderess, she is a murderess. Save us! Stop bathing!

(*The cooks stop slaughtering chickens and slaughtering suckling pigs. The bloody, desperate head lies on the floor two paces away from the body. The dog Vera howls outside the door. The police enter.*)

POLICE: Where are your parents?

CHILDREN: (*Together*) They went to the theater.

POLICE: Did they leave a long time ago?

CHILDREN: (*Together*) A long time ago, but not forever.

POLICE: And what did they go to see, a ballet or a play?

CHILDREN: (*Together*) Must be a ballet. We love our mother.

POLICE: It is pleasant to meet cultured people.

CHILDREN: (*Together*) Do you always wear sandals?

POLICE: Always. We saw the separate head and body. Here a human being lies pointlessly, herself pointless. What happened here?

CHILDREN: (*Together*) The nurse cut off the head of our dear sister with an axe.

POLICE: And where is the murderess?

NURSE: I am here before you. Tie me up, lay me down, and execute me.

POLICE: Servants, bring light.

SERVANTS: We cry violently, and the light burns.

NURSE: (*Weeping*) Sentence the horse; have pity on me.

POLICE: Why sentence the horse? The horse is not guilty of this bloodshed. We can't even find a guilty horse.

NURSE: I'm insane.

POLICE: Well, get dressed. They'll figure it out over there. Experts will examine you. Put handcuffs or chains on her.

FIRST COOK: Here, nurse, chains for your hands.

SECOND COOK: Murderess!

POLICE: Quiet, cooks. Well, well, come along. So long, children. (*Knocking on the door. Mr. and Mrs. Puzyrov rush in. They are driven insane by their grief. They shout, wail, and bellow horribly. On the wall, to the left of the door, hangs a clock, which shows midnight.*)

End of Scene i

Scene ii

(*The same evening. A forest. So much snow, one could carry it off in carts. And in fact it is being carted. In the forest, woodcutters are cutting Christmas trees. Tomorrow many Russian and European families will have Christmas trees. Among the woodcutters, one whom they call Fyodor stands out. He is the fiancé of the nurse who committed the murder.*)

What does he know about it? He knows nothing about it.
He is cutting down a tree which is to be the Christmas tree for
the Puzyrov family. All the animals have hidden away in
their lairs. The woodcutters, in chorus, sing a hymn. On the
same clock to the left of the door, the same 9:00 P.M.)

WOODCUTTERS:
> How beautiful it is in the woods
> How bright the snow.
> Pray to the wheel
> It is rounder than anything.
> The trees lie silent
> On the horses' backs.
> The children in sleds
> Squeal angelically.
> Tomorrow is Christmas
> And we unhappy folk
> In its honor
>> Will drink many a cup.
> God looks down from his throne,
> Gently smiling,
> "Ah," he sighs quietly,
> "People, you are my orphans."

FYODOR: (*Pensively*) No, you don't know what I am about to
tell you. I have a fiancée. She works as a nurse for the great
Puzyrov family. She is very beautiful. I love her very much.
She and I, we are already living together like man and wife.

WOODCUTTERS: (*Each, to the extent of his ability, shows how
much what he told them interests him. This makes it clear*

*that they are unable to talk. The fact that just a minute
ago they were singing a hymn—that is simply an accident
of the kind life is full of.)*

FYODOR: Only she is very high-strung, that fiancée of mine. What can you do? Her job is hard. It is a large family. Many children. What can you do?

WOODCUTTER: A fruit. (*He did speak, but what he said was out of turn. So it doesn't count. His pals always talk out of turn.*)

SECOND WOODCUTTER: Jaundice.

FYODOR: After I have had her I never feel bored, and I don't feel disgusted. That is because we love each other. Our souls are akin.

THIRD WOODCUTTER: Suspenders.

FYODOR: Now I am going to cart away the tree, and tonight I shall go to see her. She has bathed the children and now is waiting for me. What can one do?

(Fyodor and the woodcutters sit down on the sled and ride out of the forest. Animals come out. A giraffe, a wonderful animal; a wolf, a beaver-like animal; a lion, the king; and the porky suckling pig.)

GIRAFFE: The clock is going.

WOLF: Like a herd of sheep.

LION: Like a herd of bulls.

PORKISH SUCKLING PIG: Like sturgeon gristle.

GIRAFFE: The stars shine.

WOLF: Like the blood of sheep.

LION: Like the blood of bulls.

PIGLET: Like the milk of a wet nurse.

GIRAFFE: Rivers flow.

WOLF: Like the words of sheep.

LION: Like the words of bulls.
PIGLET: Like the goddess salmon.
GIRAFFE: Where is our death?
WOLF: In the souls of sheep.
LION: In the souls of bulls.
PIGLET: In the spacious vessels.
GIRAFFE: Thank you. The lesson is finished.
*(The animals—the giraffe, the wonderful animal; the wolf,
the beaver-like animal; the lion, the king; and the piglet, just as
he is in real life—exeunt. The forest remains alone. The
clock to the left of the door shows midnight.)*

End of Scene ii

Scene iii

*(Night. Coffin. Candles float down river. Father Puzyrov.
Glasses. Beard. Saliva. Tears. Mother Puzyrov. She wears
feminine adornments. She is a beauty. She has a bust.
Sonia Ostrova lies prone in the coffin. She is white. Her cut-off
head lies on a cushion placed close to her body. A clock hangs
on the wall to the left of the door. It shows 2:00 A.M.)*
FATHER PUZYROV: *(Cries)* My girl, Sonia, how did it happen,
   how did it happen? In the morning you were still playing
   with a ball and running around alive.
MOTHER PUZYROV: Sonechka, Sonechka, Sonechka, Sonechka,
   Sonechka, Sonechka, Sonechka.
FATHER P.: *(Weeping)* The devil made us go to the theater
   and look at that awful ballet with hairy, fat-bellied ballet
   dancers. As I now remember, one of them, as she was
   jumping around, glowingly smiled at me, but I thought to

myself: "What do I need you for? I have children; I have a wife; I have money." I was so happy. Then we left the theater, and I called the cab driver and told him, "Vania, take us home fast: I feel a little worried."

MOTHER P.: (*Yawning*) Oh cruel God, oh cruel God, why are you punishing us?

FATHER P.: (*Blowing his nose*) We were like a flame, and you are putting us out.

MOTHER P.: (*Powdering herself*) We wanted to decorate the Christmas tree for the children.

FATHER P.: (*Kisses her*) And we will decorate it, we will, despite everything.

MOTHER P.: (*Undressing*) And it will be some Christmas tree, the Christmas tree of all Christmas trees.

FATHER P.: (*Getting excited*) You are so beautiful, and the children are so dear.

MOTHER P.: (*Giving herself up to him*) God, why does the couch creak so? How awful that is.

FATHER P.: (*Finishing his business, cries*) God, our daughter has died, and we are acting like animals.

MOTHER P.: (*Crying*) She didn't die; she didn't die. That is the point; they killed her.

(*Enter a nurse, carrying 1-year-old Petya Perov.*)

NURSE: The boy woke up. He is worried about something. He is frowning. He looks at everything with revulsion.

MOTHER P.: Sleep, Petenka, sleep. We are watching over you.

PETYA PEROV, 1-year-old boy: But Sonia is still dead.

FATHER P.: (*Sighing*) Yes, she is dead. Yes, she has been killed. Yes, she is dead.

PETYA PEROV, 1-year-old boy: That's what I thought. And will there be Christmas?

MOTHER P.: There will be, there will be. What are you
children all doing now?

PETYA PEROV, 1-year-old boy: All of us children are sleeping
now. I too am falling asleep.

*(He falls asleep. The nurse carries him to his parents, who
make the sign of the cross over him and kiss him. The nurse
takes him away.)*

FATHER P.: *(To his wife)* Stay alone for while at the coffin. I'll
come back right away. I'll go and see if they aren't bringing
the Christmas tree. *(He runs out of the living room. He
returns in a second, wiping his hands.)* We must bring
candles; these have already burned down. *(He bows low to
the coffin and to his wife and leaves on tiptoe.)*

MOTHER P.: *(Alone)* Sonechka, you know, when we were going
up the stairs, a black crow was flying above me all the
time, and I felt my heart tightening with sorrow. And when
we came into the apartment and when the servant
Stephen Nikolaev said, "She's been killed. She's been killed,"
I cried out in a dull voice. I felt so terrible. So terrible.
So heavy.

*(Sonia [formerly a 32-year-old girl] lies like a railway post
that has been knocked over. Can she hear what her mother is
saying? How can she? She is quite dead. She has been killed.
The door opens. Father enters, followed by Fyodor,
followed by woodcutters. They carry in a Christmas tree. They
see the coffin, and all take off their caps. Except for the tree,
which has no cap and which understands nothing about it all.)*

FATHER P.: Quiet, brothers, quiet. Here is my daughter, a girl
breathing her last. But anyway *(he sobs)* it is not even her
last breath; her head is cut off.

FYODOR: You're telling us a sad thing, but we brought you a happy thing. Here, we brought a Christmas tree.

FIRST WOODCUTTER: Fruit.

SECOND WOODCUTTER: An epistle to butterfly eggs.

THIRD WOODCUTTER: A man is drowning. Save him.

(All leave. Sonia, the former 32-year-old girl, remains alone. Her head and her body remain.)

THE HEAD: Body, you heard everything.

THE BODY: I heard nothing. I have no ears. But I felt it all.

End of Scene iii

End of Act I

Act II

Scene iv [2]

(Police station. Night. On the clock to the left of door, midnight. A clerk and a policeman sitting.)

CLERK: Sealing wax has always had a hot breast. The quill pen has two beautiful hips.

POLICEMAN: I'm bored, clerk. All day I stood guard with my mind blank. I froze through and through. I became chilled. Everything in me became chilled. The wandering rain and Egyptian pyramids in sunny Egypt. Cheer me up!

CLERK: You are a policeman. I see you have gone out of your mind. Why should I cheer you up? I am your boss.

---

[2] Vvedensky numbers the scenes consecutively throughout the play. —Ed.

POLICEMAN: Oh, God, pharmacies, taverns, and brothels will some day make me lose my mind. Why should I be taking poisoned people to the pharmacies? I should prefer to sit in the library. Read various passages from Marx, and in the morning drink, not water, but cream.

CLERK: Those drunks—there he is, swinging around.

POLICEMAN:

> He is swinging around like this pendulum.
> And the Milky Way is swinging above him.
> How many there are of those toilers of the sea,
> Cast-down people and peasant serfs.

(*Enter a district police officer and gendarmes.*)

DISTRICT POLICE OFFICER: Everybody stand up. Clear everything away. Pray to God. They are bringing a woman criminal here.

(*Soldiers, servants, cooks, teachers of Latin and Greek drag in the nurse who killed Sonia Ostrova.*)

POLICE OFFICER: Leave her. (*Turning to the nurse*) You'll get locked up.

NURSE: My hands are covered with blood. My teeth are covered with blood. God has abandoned me. I am insane. What is she doing now?

POLICE OFFICER: You, nurse, who are you talking about? Look, make sure you don't talk off the subject. Give me a glass of vodka. Who is the "she" you mean?

NURSE: Sonia Ostrova, whom I cut up. What is she thinking now? I feel cold. My head and stomach hurt.

CLERK: Still a young woman, still not ugly, still good, still like a star, still like a string, still like a soul.

POLICEMAN: (*To the nurse*)

> I can imagine your state of mind,
> You killed the girl with an axe.
> And your soul now bears suffering
> That a pen cannot describe.

POLICE OFFICER: Well, nurse, how do you feel now? Is it pleasant to be a murderess?

NURSE: No, it's depressing.

OFFICER: They'll execute you. By God, they'll execute you.

NURSE: I beat my arms; I beat my legs; her head is in my head; I am Sonia Ostrova; the nurse cut me down. Fedya, Fyodor, save me.

POLICEMAN:

> I remember once upon a time I stood guard in the
> freezing cold.
> People went by, around me animals dashed by.
> A cloud of Greek horsemen went by on the boulevard
> like a shadow.
> I blew my whistle. Called the janitors.
> For a long time we all stood there and looked through
> a telescope.
> We put our ears to the ground, listened for the hoof
> beats.
> Woe to us, in vain we looked for the army of horsemen.
> Quietly weeping we went to our homes.

OFFICER: Why did you tell us that? I ask you. You fool! Climber! You don't know the civil service.

POLICEMAN: I wanted to distract the murderess from her dark, gloomy thoughts.

CLERK: Someone is knocking. It is the medics. Medics, take her to your lunatic asylum.

MEDIC: Whom should we take—that Napoleon?

(Exeunt. The clock to the left of the door shows 4:00 A.M.)

End of Scene iv

Scene v

(Insane asylum. A doctor is standing near the parapet and is aiming at a mirror. Around him, flowers, pictures, rugs. The clock to the left of the door shows 4:00 A.M.)

DOCTOR: Lord, how awful. Everyone around here is insane. They are persecuting me. They are devouring my dreams. They want to shoot me. Here is one of them; he sneaked up and is aiming at me. He is aiming, but he is not shooting. He is not shooting. He is not shooting. He is not shooting, but he is aiming at me. I'll shoot him.

(He shoots. The mirror breaks. Enter a stony-faced attendant.)

ATTENDANT: Who fired the gun?

DOCTOR: I don't know; I think the mirror. How many of you are there?

ATTENDANT: There are many of us.

DOCTOR: Well, well. My nonsense hurts a little. They have brought someone over there.

ATTENDANT: They have brought the murderess-nurse from the police station.

DOCTOR: She is black as coal.

ATTENDANT: You know, I don't know everything.

DOCTOR: How now? I don't like this little rug. (*He shoots at it.*

The attendant falls as though dead.) Why did you fall down? I did not shoot you but the rug.

ATTENDANT: (*Rises.*) It seemed to me that I was the rug. I made a mistake. The nurse says she is insane.

DOCTOR: She is the one who says that; we don't say that. We won't say that idly. You know, I am holding all our grounds—the park with all its trees and its worms underground and its soundless clouds—I am holding them here, here—well, what is it called? (*He points to the palm of his hand.*)

ATTENDANT: Grapes.

DOCTOR: No.

ATTENDANT: Wall.

DOCTOR: No. In the palm of my hand. Well, bring in that nurse.

(The nurse enters.)

NURSE: I'm insane. I killed a child.

DOCTOR: It's not good to kill children. You are sane.

NURSE: I didn't do it on purpose. I'm insane. They can execute me. . . .

DOCTOR: You are sane. You have a good color in your face. Count up to three.

NURSE: I don't know how.

ATTENDANT: One, two, three.

DOCTOR: You see, and you say you don't know how. You have an iron constitution.

NURSE: I'm in despair. It was not I who was counting, but your attendant.

DOCTOR: Now it is too late to be sure. You hear me.

ATTENDANT: I hear you. I am the nurse; I must hear everything.

NURSE: Oh, God, my life is over. Soon they will execute me.

DOCTOR: Take her away, and bring the Christmas tree. God, that is better. A tiny bit more cheerful. I'm fed up with being on duty. Good night. (*Patients sail away out of the room in a boat, pushing themselves along the floor with oars.*) Good morning, patients, where are you going?

LUNATICS: To pick berries, to pick mushrooms.

DOCTOR: Oh, I see.

ATTENDANT: And I'll go with you to swim.

DOCTOR: Nurse, go have yourself executed. You are sane. You are a picture of good health.

(*Clock to the left of the door shows 6:00 A.M.*)

End of Scene v

Scene vi

(*Corridor, doors here, doors there. Here too. Dark. Fyodor the woodcutter, friend of the nurse who murdered Sonia, in a coat with tails, carrying candy in his hand, walks along the corridor. For no good reason he is blindfolded. The clock to the left of the door shows 5:00 A.M.*)

FYODOR: (*Entering through one door*) You're sleeping?

VOICE OF A MAID: I'm sleeping, but come in.

FYODOR: That means you're in bed. Look, I brought a present.

MAID: Where are you coming from?

FYODOR: I was in the public steam baths. I washed myself with brushes like a horse. They blindfolded me there for a joke. I'll take off my coat.

MAID: Get undressed; lie down on top of me.

FYODOR: I will, I will. Don't hurry. Eat my present.

MAID: I am eating it. And you do your business. Tomorrow we are going to have Christmas.

FYODOR: (*Lies down on top of her.*) I know, I know.

MAID: And our girl got killed.

FYODOR: I know. I heard about it.

MAID: She is already lying in her coffin.

FYODOR: I know, I know.

MAID: Her mother cried, and her father did too.

FYODOR: (*Gets up off her.*) It's boring for me to be with you. You are not my fiancée.

MAID: So what?

FYODOR: You are a stranger to me spiritually. Soon I'll vanish like a poppy.

MAID: Do I need you badly? Besides, do you want to do it one more time?

FYODOR: No, no, I feel terribly sad. Soon I'm going to vanish like happiness.

MAID: What are you thinking about right now?

FYODOR: I'm thinking that the whole world has become uninteresting to me after you. I've lost the salt, the walls, the window, and the sky, and the forest. Soon I'll vanish like the night.

MAID: You're impolite. I'll punish you for that. Look at me. I'll tell you something unnatural.

FYODOR: Try it. You're a toad.

MAID: Your fiancée killed a girl. You saw the murdered girl. Your fiancée cut off her head.

FYODOR: (*Croaks.*)

MAID: (*Laughing*) You know Sonia Ostrova. Well, it is her that she killed.

FYODOR: (*Miaows.*)

MAID: What is bitter to you?

FYODOR: (*Whistles like a bird.*)

MAID: Well, and you loved her. Why? What for? You probably did it yourself.

FYODOR: No, not myself.

MAID: Go on, go on, I don't believe you.

FYODOR: Word of honor.

MAID: Go away now. I want to sleep. Tomorrow will be Christmas.

FYODOR: I know, I know.

MAID: Why are you repeating yourself again? You have no longer anything to do with me.

FYODOR: I repeat myself because of my great grief. What else have I got left?

MAID: Grieve, grieve, grieve. All the same, nothing will help you any.

FYODOR: Nothing will help me, anyway. You're right.

MAID: Maybe you'll try to study.

FYODOR: I will try. I'll study Latin. I'll become a teacher. Good-by.

MAID: Good-by.

(*Fyodor vanishes. The maid sleeps. The clock to the left of the door shows 6:00 A.M.*)

End of Scene vi
End of Act II

Act III

Scene vii

(Table. A coffin on the table. In the coffin, Sonia Ostrova.
Inside Sonia Ostrova, a heart. In the heart, coagulating blood.
In the blood, red and white corpuscles. Also of course gangrene
poison. Everybody sees that it is dawn. Vera, the dog, lifting
its tail, walks around the coffin. The clock to the left of the door
shows 8:00 A.M.)

DOG VERA:

> I walk around the coffin
> I look around with both eyes,
> This death is a test.
>
> Poor people pray to bread
> The bronze people pray to the sky
> The priest will say Mass here.
>
> The corpse lies there stiffening
> I had a sweet tooth for ham
> Dulcinea is dead.
>
> Everywhere bloody spots
> What black manners
> Nurse, no, you are not right.
>
> Life is given for decoration
> Death is given for fright
> What is destruction for?

What are your criteria
The most important arteries
And the boldest bacterias?

Fyodor would stroke your belly
Every morning he would stroke it
And now you yourself will become a corpse.

(One-year-old boy enters, babbling.)

PETYA PEROV, 1-year old boy: I'm the youngest of all. I wake up earlier than anybody. Two years ago I couldn't remember anything the way I remember things now. I hear the dog reciting a speech in verse. She is crying so quietly.

DOG VERA: How cold it is in the room. What did you say, Petya?

PETYA PEROV, 1-year-old boy: What can I say? I can only communicate some things.

DOG VERA: I wail, wail. Wishing to see Sonia alive, alive, alive.

PETYA PEROV, 1-year-old boy: She was unusually bad-mannered. Now it is terrible to look at her.

DOG VERA: You are not surprised that I am talking and not barking?

PETYA PEROV, 1-year-old boy: What can surprise me, at my age? Calm down.

DOG VERA: Give me a glass of water. It's too much for me.

PETYA PEROV, 1-year-old boy: Don't get excited. In my short life I have not yet become acquainted with that.

DOG VERA: This wretched Sonia Ostrova was immoral. But I showed her. Explain everything to me.

PETYA PEROV, 1-year-old boy: Papa, Mama, Uncle, Auntie, Nursie, Daddy, Mummy.

Dog Vera: What are you saying? Pull yourself together.

Petya Perov, 1-year-old boy: I'm one year old. Don't forget it. Daddy, Mummy, Uncle, Auntie, fire, cloud, apple, stone. Don't forget it. *(Dirties his pants while on the nurse's lap.)*

Dog Vera: *(Recalling)* He really is still small and young. *(Misha Pestrov and Dunya Shustrova enter, mumbling, with their hands over their mouths.)*

Misha Pestrov, 76-year-old boy: Best wishes. Happy Christmas. Soon there will be a Christmas pee.

Dunya Shustrova, 82-year-old girl: Not pee but bee. Not bee but tree. Best wishes. Is Sonia sleeping?

Dog Vera: No. She is peeing.

(Clock to the left of door shows 9:00 A.M.)

End of Scene vii

Scene viii

(A courtroom painted on a back drop. Court employees dressed like old people. Court employees with wigs. Insects jump around. Mothballs smell strong. Gendarmes puffing up. The clock to the left of the door shows 8:00 A.M.)

Judge: *(Expiring)* I'm dying, not living till Christmas. *(They quickly replace him with another judge.)*

Second Judge: I feel bad, I feel bad. Save me. *(He dies. They quickly replace him with another judge.)*

All: *(Chorus)*

  We are frightened by these two deaths—
  It is a very rare happening.
  This happens very seldom—judge for yourselves.

All the Others: *(In turn)*

  We judge.

By judging.
To judge.
To wake up.
They carry
   The court and the
   Vessel of people
They carry
   On the dish
   On the vessel
   Of judges.

(The court goes into session and begins to hear the case of Kozlov and Oslov.)

SECRETARY: *(Reads the protocol)*
   One winter evening
   Kozlov went to the river to give the goats a bath.
   He sees Oslov coming
   He brings donkeys from the river.

   Oslov says to Kozlov,
   "You believe a word of honor
   Vainly you bring goats to bathe
   Did you read the Chasoslov?"

[*Eight more nonsense quatrains have been omitted.*—Ed.]

JUDGES: The symptom of death is evident.
SECRETARY: Well, evident.
JUDGES: *(Softly)* Don't say "well."
SECRETARY: All right, I won't.
JUDGE: I begin the trial.

I judge
I cut
I sit
I rage
No, I don't sin.

One more time.

I judge
I cut
I sit
No, I don't sin.

One more time.

I judge
I cut
I sit
No, I don't sin.

I have done judging; all is clear to me. Adelina Frantsevna
Shmetterling, a nurse, who killed Sonia Ostrova, sentenced
to be executed by hanging.

NURSE: *(Shouts)* I cannot live.

SECRETARY: Well, you will not live. We are meeting you
halfway.

*(It is clear to everybody that the nurse was present at the court
trial, and that the conversation of Kozlov and Oslov was
carried on merely to distract people's attention. The clock to
the left of the door shows 9:00 A.M.)*

End of Scene viii
End of Act III

Act IV

Scene ix

(The ninth scene, like all the preceding ones, represents events which took place six years before my birth, or forty years ago. That is the least of it. So why should we grieve and weep that somebody was killed? We didn't know any of them, and anyway they have all died. Between the third and fourth acts a few hours passed. A group of children stand before tightly closed doors—clean-washed, decorated doors. The clock to the left of the door shows 6:00 P.M.)

PETYA PEROV, 1-year-old boy: They are going to open right away. They are going to open right away. How interesting. I will see the Christmas tree.

NINA SEROVA, 8-year-old girl: You saw it last year too.

PETYA PEROV, 1-year-old boy: I saw it. I saw it. But I don't remember it. I'm still small. I'm still stupid.

VARYA PETROVA, 17-year-old girl: O Christmas tree, O Christmas tree. O Christmas tree.

DUNYA SHUSTROVA, 82-year-old girl: I'll run around it and I'll laugh and laugh.

VOLODYA KOMAROV, 25-year-old boy: Nanny, I want to go to the bathroom.

NANNY: When you need to go to the bathroom, say it very quietly or you'll embarrass the girls.

MISHA PESTROV, 76-year-old boy: Do girls go to the bathroom?

NANNY: Yes, they do, they do.

Misha Pestrov, 76-year-old boy: How do they go? How? And you go too?

Nanny: They go the way they need to; that's how they go. And I go too.

Volodya Komarov, 25-year-old boy: There, now I have been already. I feel better now. Soon they will let us in.

Varya Petrova, 17-year-old girl: *(Whispering)* Nanny, I need to go too. I feel tense.

Nanny: *(Whispering)* Make believe you are going.

Misha Pestrov, 76-year-old boy: Where would she go with you?

Girls: *(All together)* Where the tsar goes on foot. *(They cry and stay.)*

Nanny: You fools. You should have said you were going to play the piano.

Petya Petrov, 1-year-old boy: Why are you teaching them to lie? What is the use of such lying? How dreary life is, no matter what they tell us.

(Suddenly the door opens. The parents stand in the doorway.)

Father P.: Well, come and have a good time. I did what I could. Here is the Christmas tree. Now mother will play.

Mother P.: *(She sits down at the piano, plays, and sings)*
Music resounds
    Like a sword against granite
All open the door
    And we enter Tver
Not Tver but simply a room
Filled with a Christmas tree.
All hide the sting of anger
    One flies like a bee

Another like a butterfly
    Above the Christmas tree like a stalk
    And the third like a fireplace
    The fourth like chalk
    The fifth climbs up the candle
    Hollers, and I too, I holler.

PETYA PEROV, 1-year-old boy: Christmas tree, I must tell you
    how beautiful you are.
NINA SEROVA, 8-year-old girl: Tree, I want to declare to you
    how good you are.
VARYA PETROVA, 17-year-old girl: O tree, O tree, O tree, O tree,
    O tree, O tree.
VOLODYA KOMAROV, 25-year-old boy: Tree, I want to tell you
    how marvelous you are.
MISHA PESTROV, 76-year-old boy: Happiness, happiness,
    happiness, happiness, happiness.
DUNYA SHUSTROVA, 82-year-old girl: What teeth. What teeth.
    What teeth.
FATHER P.: I'm very glad that everybody is happy. I'm very
    unhappy that Sonia died. How sad, how sad for everybody.
MOTHER P.: *(Sings)*

    A o u e i ya
    V G R T.
(Can't continue singing; weeps.)

VOLODYA KOMAROV, 25-year-old boy: *(Shoots himself in the
    temple, above the ear.)* Mother, don't cry. Laugh. I too have
    shot myself.
MOTHER P.: *(Sings)* Very well, I'm not going to spoil all your

good time. Let us have a good time. But still, poor, poor
Sonia.

PETYA PEROV, 1-year-old boy: Never mind, never mind, Mother.
Life will pass quickly. Soon we'll all die.

MOTHER P.: Petya, you're joking. What are you saying?

FATHER P.: It seems he's not joking. Volodya Komarov has also
died.

MOTHER P.: He didn't die, did he?

FATHER P.: But of course. Why, he shot himself.

DUNYA SHUSTROVA, 82-year-old girl: I'm dying, sitting in the
armchair.

MOTHER P.: What is she saying?

MISHA PESTROV, 76-year-old boy: I wanted longevity. There is
no longevity. *(He dies.)*

NANNY: Children's diseases, children's diseases. When will
they ever learn how to conquer them? *(She dies.)*

NINA SEROVA, 8-year-old girl: *(Weeps)* Nanny, Nanny, what is
the matter with you? Why do you have such a sharp-pointed
nose.

PETYA PEROV, 1-year-old boy: Her nose is sharp, but a knife or
razor is still sharper.

FATHER P.: Two little children are still left to us. Petya and
Nina. Well, we'll carry on somehow.

MOTHER P.: That cannot console me. Why is the sun shining
outside the window?

FATHER P.: What sun? It's night now. We'll put out the lights
on the Christmas tree.

PETYA PEROV, 1-year-old boy: How I feel like dying. Simply
passionately. I'm dying. I'm dying. So I have died.

NINA SEROVA, 8-year-old girl: Christmas tree, Christmas tree,

Christmas tree, Christmas tree, Christmas tree, Christmas tree. I've died.

FATHER P.: They've died too. They say the woodcutter Fyodor has finished his studies and become a teacher of Latin. What has happened to me? A stabbing in the heart. I see nothing. I'm dying.

MOTHER P.: What are you saying? You see there is a man of the common people, and he's worked his way up. God, what an unhappy Christmas we're having. *(She falls down and dies.)*

End of Scene ix
End of Act IV
AND OF THE WHOLE PLAY
(The clock to the left of the door is blank.)

APPENDIX

The Oberiu Manifesto [1]

Oberiu (The Association for Real Art) works with the House of the Press and unites those working in all forms of art who accept its program and apply it in their work. [2]

Oberiu is divided into four sections: literature, fine arts, theater, and cinema. The fine-arts section carries on its work in experimental ways; the other sections are presented at evening programs, in stage productions, and in print. At this time Oberiu is organizing a musical section.

The Social Role of Oberiu

The great revolutionary shift in culture and the conditions of everyday life so characteristic of our age is being impeded in the area of art by many abnormal phenomena. We have not yet completely understood the undeniable truth that the proletariat cannot be satisfied in the area of art with the artistic method of old schools, that its artistic principles go much deeper and undermine old art at the roots. It is ridiculous to think that when Repin is painting the year 1905, he is a revolutionary artist. It is still more ridiculous to think that all AKHRR's [Associations of Artists of Revolutionary Russia] bear within themselves the seeds of a new proletarian art.

---

[1] The circumstances of publication are explained in the Introduction. —Ed.

[2] *Oberiu* was a word made up out of the initial sounds of the words for Association for Real Art (Ob'edinenie Real'nogo Iskusstva). The sound *u* was added at the end just for fun.—Ed.

We welcome the demand for a universally intelligible art comprehensible in its form even to a village schoolboy, but the demand for only such art leads into a maze of the most terrible mistakes. As a result we have heaps of literary trash overflowing in book warehouses, while the reading public of the first proletarian state reads translations of Western bourgeois writers.

We understand very well that it is impossible to find a single correct solution for the situation that has developed. But we do not understand at all why a number of artistic schools which work tenaciously, honestly, and persistently in this area are pushed, as it were, to the back alleys of art, at a time when they ought to be supported in every way by the entire Soviet community. We do not understand why the school of Filonov has been pushed out of the Academy, why Malevich cannot carry on his architectural work in the USSR, why Terentev's *Inspector General* was so badly received. We do not understand why so-called leftist art, which has not a few merits and achievements to its credit, is considered to be hopeless junk and, still worse, charlatanism. How much inner dishonesty, how much artistic bankruptcy is concealed in such a wild approach.

Oberiu now comes forward as a new section of leftist revolutionary art. Oberiu does not concern itself with only the subject matter and the high points of artistic work; it seeks an organically new concept of life and approach to things. Oberiu penetrates into the center of the word, of dramatic action, and of the film frame.

The new artistic method of Oberiu is universal. It finds a

way to represent any subject. Oberiu is revolutionary precisely by virtue of this method.

We are not so presumptuous as to regard our work as completed. But we are firmly convinced that a strong foundation has been laid and that we have enough strength to build further. We believe and know that only the left course in art will lead us to the highway to the new proletarian artistic culture.

Poetry of the Oberiuty

Who are we? And why do we exist? We, the Oberiuty, are honest workers in art. We are poets of a new world view and of a new art. We are not only creators of a poetic language, but also founders of a new feeling for life and its objects. Our will to create is universal. It spans all genres of art and penetrates life, grasping it from all sides. The world covered by the rubbish of the tongues of a multitude of fools bogged down in the mire of "experiences" and "emotions" is now being reborn in all the purity of concrete, bold forms. Some people even now call us *zaumniki*.[3] It is difficult to decide whether that is because of a complete misunderstanding or a hopeless failure to grasp the principles of literary art. No school is more hostile to us than *zaum*. We, people who are real and concrete to the marrow of our bones, are the first enemies of those who castrate the word and make it into a powerless and senseless mongrel. In our work we broaden the meaning of the object

---

[3] *Zaumniki* (from *zaum*—"transsense"): writers who use made-up syllables and sounds, rejecting existing languages and referential meaning.—Ed.

and of the word, but we do not destroy it in any way. The concrete object, once its literary and everyday skin is peeled away, becomes a property of art. In poetry the collisions of verbal meanings express that object with the exactness of mechanical technology. Are you beginning to complain that it is not the same object you see in life? Come closer and touch it with your fingers. Look at the object with naked eyes, and you will see it cleansed for the first time of decrepit literary gilding. Maybe you will insist that our subjects are "unreal" and "illogical"? But who said that the logic of life is compulsory in art? We marvel at the beauty of a painted woman despite the fact that, contrary to anatomical logic, the artist twisted out the shoulder blade of his heroine and moved it sideways. Art has a logic of its own, and it does not destroy the object but helps us to know it.

We broaden the meaning of the object, word, and act. This work proceeds in different directions; each of us has his own creative personality, and this often confuses people. They talk about an accidental association of various people. Evidently they assume that a literary school is something like a monastery in which the monks are all exactly alike. Our association is free and voluntary. It unites masters, not apprentices; artist-painters, not wall painters. Everybody knows himself and everybody knows what links him to the others.

A. VVEDENSKY (at the extreme left of our association) breaks the object down into parts, but the object does not thereby lose its concreteness. Vvedensky breaks action down into fragments, but the action does not lose its creative order. If one were to decode it completely, the result would give the appearance of nonsense. Why appearance? Because obvious nonsense is the *zaum* word, and it is absent from Vvedensky's works. One must be more curious, not too lazy to examine the collision of word meanings. Poetry is not porridge that one swallows without chewing and forgets right away.

K. VAGINOV,[4] whose world phantasmagoria passes before our eyes as though clothed in fog and trembling. But through this fog you feel the closeness of the object and its warmth; you feel the influx of crowds and the rocking of trees which live and breathe after their own fashion, after Vaginov's fashion, for the artist has sculptured them with his own hands and warmed them with his own breath.

IGOR BAKHTEREV, a poet who finds himself in the lyrical coloring of his object material. The object and the action, broken down into their component parts, spring into being again, renewed by the spirit of new Oberiu lyricism. But lyricism here does not exist for its own sake, it is no more than the means of displacing [5] the object into the field of new artistic perception.

---

[4] The author of several books, among which particularly the novel *Goat's Song* and the volume of verse *An Attempt at Uniting Words by Means of Rhyme* are noteworthy.

[5] Displacing: the Russian word is *sdvinut'*, related to the noun *sdvig*, both very common in the terminology of Russian Futurism, Khlebnikov, and the Oberiuty. It is difficult to find an English word with the same connotations. It means a shift, a change, a push of something into something else. It is frequently used by the Oberiuty because it expresses for them a violent, decisive metamorphosis, a shifting from one plane of being or perception or representation to another—a wrenching or a yanking from one level of semantics or existence to another, a shift from one category of conventional thinking or living to another. Significantly, it is a word used in Russian for a geological fault.—Ed.

N. ZABOLOTSKY, a poet of naked concrete figures brought close to the eyes of the spectator. One must hear and read him more with one's eyes and fingers than with one's ears. The object does not crumble; on the contrary, it becomes tighter and firmer, as though to meet the feeling hand of the spectator. The development of action and the setting play a secondary role to that main task.

DANIIL KHARMS, a poet and dramatist, whose attention is concentrated, not on a static figure, but on the collision of a number of objects, on their interrelationships. At the moment of action, the object assumes new concrete traits full of real meaning. The action, turned inside out, in its new appearance still keeps a classical touch and at the same time represents a broad sweep of the Oberiu world view.

BOR. LEVIN,[6] a prose writer at present working experimentally.

Such are the broad outlines of the literary section of our association as a whole and of each of us in particular; our poems tell the rest of the story.

As people of a concrete world, object, and word—that is how we see our social significance. To cleanse the world by the movements of a hand, to cleanse the object of the rubbish of ancient putrefied cultures—are these not the real needs of our time? It is for that reason that our association bears the name Oberiu—Association for Real Art.

---

[6] Probably the same Boris Levin whom Marshak, according to Harrison Salisbury, nicknamed "a Himalayan bear," and who was killed early in World War II in a Nazi attack during his first night in a dugout. See Harrison E. Salisbury, *The 900 Days: The Siege of Leningrad* (New York, 1969), p. 175. He is probably the same man as Doycber Levin, mentioned on pages 10 and 20.

On the Road to a New Cinema

The film has, up to now, not existed as an independent art. It has been a combination of old "arts," and at best there have been isolated timid attempts to chart new paths in the search for a real language of the film. That is how it has been.

Now the time has come for the cinema to find its own real face, its own means of making an impression, and its own—really its own—language. Nobody is able to "discover" the cinematography of the future, and we are not promising to do that. Time will do that for us.

But to experiment, to search for ways to a new cinema, and to strengthen some new artistic steps—that is the duty of every honest cinematographer. And we are doing that.

In a short note there is not space to tell in detail about all our work. Let us now say only a few words about "Film No. 1," which is already finished. In the cinema, the time for subjects (themes) is past. Adventure films and comedies, precisely because they have subjects, are now the most unfilmlike genres. When the subjects (the action, the plot) are self-sufficient, they subordinate the material. The finding of autonomous, specific material is in itself already a key to the finding of the language of the film. "Film No. 1" is the first stage of our experimental work. The plot is not important to us. Important to us is the "atmosphere" of the material, of the subject chosen by us. Separate elements of the film can be completely unconnected as far as plot and meaning are concerned. They can be antipodal. We repeat, that is not the point. The whole essence is in the atmosphere peculiar to the given material—the subject. Our main concern is to bring to light that atmosphere.

How we solve this problem can be understood most easily when we see the films on the screen.

On January 24 of this year, in the House of the Press, we shall give a program. There we shall show a film and tell in detail about our searches and orientations. The film was made by the makers of "Film No. 1"—Alexander Razumovsky and Klementy Mints.

The Oberiu Theater

Suppose two people walk out on the stage, say nothing, but tell each other something by signs. While they are doing that, they are solemnly puffing out their cheeks. The spectators laugh. Is this theater? Yes, it is. You may say it is *balagan*.[7] But *balagan* is theater.

Or suppose a canvas is let down on the stage. On the canvas is a picture of a village. The stage is dark. Then it begins to get lighter. A man dressed as a shepherd walks onstage and plays on a pipe. Is that theater? Yes.

A chair appears on the stage; on the chair is a samovar. The samovar boils. Instead of steam, naked arms rise up from under the lid.

All these—the man and his movements on the stage, the boiling samovar, the village painted on the canvas, the light getting dimmer and getting brighter—all these are separate elements of theater.

Until now, all these elements have been subordinated to the dramatic plot—to the play. A play has been a story, told through characters, about some kind of event. On the stage, all

---

[7] *Balagan:* Punch and Judy show; booth show at a fair.—Ed.

have worked to explain the meaning and course of that event more clearly, more intelligibly, and to relate it more closely to life.

That is not at all what the theater is. If an actor who represents a minister begins to move around on the stage on all fours and howls like a wolf, or an actor who represents a Russian peasant suddenly delivers a long speech in Latin—that will be theater, that will interest the spectator, even if it takes place without any relation to a dramatic plot. Such an action will be a separate item; a series of such items organized by the director will make up a theatrical performance, which will have its plot line and its scenic meaning.

This will be a plot which only the theater can give. The plots of theatrical performances are theatrical, just as the plots of musical works are musical. All represent one thing—a world of appearances—but depending on the material, they render it differently, after their own fashion.

When you come to us, forget everything that you have been accustomed to seeing in all theaters. Maybe a great deal will seem ridiculous. We take a dramatic plot. We develop it slowly at first; then suddenly it is interrupted by seemingly extraneous and clearly ridiculous elements. You are surprised. You want to find that customary logical sequence of connections which, it seems to you, you see in life. But it is not there. Why not? Because an object and a phenomenon transported from life to the stage lose their lifelike sequence of connections and acquire another—a theatrical one. We are not going to explain it. In order to understand the sequence of connections of any theatrical performance one must see it. We can only say that our task is to render the world of concrete objects on the stage in their interrelationships and collisions. We worked to solve this task in our production of "Elizabeth Bam."

"Elizabeth Bam" was written on commission for the theatrical section of Oberiu by one of the members, D. Kharms. The dramatic plot of the play is shattered by many seemingly extraneous subjects which detach the object as a separate whole, existing outside its connection with others. Therefore the dramatic plot does not arise before the spectator as a clear plot image; it glimmers, so to speak, behind the back of the action. The dramatic plot is replaced by a scenic plot which arises spontaneously from all the elements of our spectacle. The center of our attention is on it. But at the same time, separate elements of the spectacle are equally valuable and important to us. They live their separate lives without subordinating themselves to the ticking of the theatrical metronome. Here a corner of a gold frame sticks out—it lives as an object of art; there a fragment of a poem is recited—it is autonomous in its significance, and at the same time, independent of its will, it advances the scenic plot of the play. The scenery, the movement of an actor, a bottle thrown down, the train of a costume—they are actors, just like those who shake their heads and speak various words and phrases.

The structure of the performance was worked out by I. Bakhterev, Bor. Levin, and Daniil Kharms. Staging: I. Bakhterev.

A BIBLIOGRAPHICAL NOTE

Various short prose pieces and excerpts from Kharms's notebooks
have been published in the Moscow newspaper *Literaturnaya
gazeta:* "Anekdoty iz zhizni Pushkina" ("Anecdotes about Pushkin's
Life"), 1, 2, 3, and 6 (No. 47, 1967); "P'esa" ("A Play"), "Simfonia
No. 2," and "Iz zapisnoy knizhki" ("From a Notebook") (No. 46,
1968); and "Svyaz'" ("The Connection") and "Basnya" ("A
Fable") (No. 27, 1970).

Two volumes of poetry by various poets—*Sobranie stikhotvorenii,
Leningradskoe otdelenie Vserossiyskogo soyuza poetov* ("Collection
of Poems, the Leningrad Division of the All-Russian Association of
Poets") (Leningrad, 1926); and *Kostyor: Sbornik, Leningradsky
soyuz poetov* ("Bonfire: Anthology, the Leningrad Association of
Poets") (Leningrad, 1927)—each published one poem by Kharms
and one by Vvedensky. The 1926 volume published Kharms's poem
"Sluchay na zheleznoy doroge" ("Incident on the Railway") and
Vvedensky's "Nachalo poemy" ("Beginning of a Long Poem"). The
1927 volume included Kharms's "Stikh Petra Yashina" ("Peter
Yashin's Verse") and Vvedensky's "No vopli trudnykh anglichan"
("Difficult Englishmen's Screams"). "Incident on the Railway" has
been reprinted in the bilingual anthology edited by Vladimir Markov
and Merrill Sparks, *Modern Russian Poetry* (Indianapolis, 1969),
pages 724–727, in the Russian original as well as in English
translation.

The anthology of poems *Den' Poezii* ("The Day of Poetry")
(Moscow, 1965) includes two poems by Kharms, "Vykhodit Mariia"
("Maria Comes Out") and "Podruga" ("Friend"), on pages 291–294.

Two poems by Vvedensky were published in Tartu (Soviet Estonia) in 1967: "Znachenie morya" ("The Significance of the Sea") and "Elegia," in *Materialy XXII Nauchnoy Studencheskoy konferentsii, Tartuskii Gosudarstvenny Universitet* ("Proceedings of the Twenty-Second Student Conference, Tartu State University"), pages 109–115. The poems follow two jointly written articles by two Leningrad scholars, Mikhail Meilakh and Anatoly Alexandrov: "Tvorchestvo Daniila Kharmsa" ("Daniil Kharms's Writings"), pages 101–104; and "Tvorchestvo A. Vvedenskogo" ("A. Vvedensky's Writings"), pages 105–109.

Many of Daniil Kharms's works for children were published in his lifetime. There is a listing in the bibliography of Soviet children's literature, *Sovietskie detskie pisateli: Bibliograficheskii slovar* ("Soviet Children's Writers: A Bibliographical Encyclopedia") (Moscow, 1961), page 385. Alexander Vvedensky's published children's works are listed on page 73.

Two volumes of selected children's stories and verses by Kharms were published in Russia in the 1960's—*Igra* ("Play") (Moscow, 1962), and *Chto eto bylo?* ("What Was That?") (Moscow, 1967). The latter volume has a brief postscript about Kharms by N. Khalatov.

English translations of four poems by Kharms were published in *M.P.T.* (*Modern Poetry in Translation*), No. 6 (1970): "Fire," "For a Long Time I Looked at the Green Trees," "Death of the Wild Warrior," and a dramatic dialogue between Nicholas II and Alexandra Fyodorovna, with a biographical note by the translator.

"The Oberiu Manifesto" was published with many annotations by R. R. Milner-Gulland, in " 'Left Art' in Leningrad: The *Oberiu* Declaration," *Oxford Slavonic Papers,* New Series III (1970).

A Polish translation of "Elizaveta Bam" was published in *Dialog* (Warsaw), No. 12 (1966). Several short prose pieces and poems by Kharms, translated into Czech by Olga Mašková, appeared in the

Prague literary magazine *Plamen* ("Flame"), No. 11 (1967), and No. 3 (1968). *Světová literatura* ("World Literature"), another Prague journal, published Václav Daněk's Czech translations of various brief works by Kharms and Vvedensky, together with a discussion of the two writers by Anatoly Alexandrov, under the title "Ignavia" (No. 6 [1968], pages 156–174). A small collection in German is Daniil Charms, *Fälle: Prosa, Szenen, Dialoge* ("Cases: Prose, Scenes, Dialogues"), translated by Peter Urban (Frankfort on the Main, 1970). English versions of six Kharms stories (with the titles "Meeting," "Anecdote Seven, Life of Pushkin," "Blue Book Number Ten," "Things You Can Get in the Food Stores These Days," "Dream," and "Symphony No. 2") are included in an English translation (in *Atlas*, September 1970, pages 56–58) of Rolf-Dieter Brinkmann's German review of the collection. The translator of the review is not named.

Several brief discussions of Kharms and Vvedensky were published in the 1960's. Very useful is Anatoly Alexandrov's article "Oberiu: Predvaritel'nye zametki" ("Oberiu: Preliminary Notes"), in the periodical *Československá rusistika*, XIII, No. 5 (1968), pages 296–303. The same author's article "Stikhotvorenie Nikolaia Zabolotskogo 'Vosstanie' " ("The Poem 'Revolution,' by Nikolai Zabolotsky"), in *Russkaya literatura*, No. 3 (1966), pages 190–195, while ostensibly dealing with Zabolotsky, is actually largely about Kharms and Vvedensky.

Other discussions are by the poet Boris Slutsky, "O Kharmse" ("About Kharms"), in the Soviet mass monthly *Yunost'* ("Youth"), No. 9 (1968), page 106; by the Zagreb University scholar Alexander Flaker, "O rasskazakh Daniila Khamsa" ("About the Stories by Daniil Kharms"), in *Československá rusistika*, XIV, No. 2 (1969), pages 78–84; and the recollections by Vladimir Lifshits, "Mozhet byt', prigoditsya" ("Maybe It Will Come in Handy"), *Voprosy literatury* ("Problems of Literature"), No. 1 (1969), pages 242–243.

Passing references can be found in A. Chukovskaya, "Marshak-redaktor" ("Marshak as Editor"), in the Soviet series *Detskaya literatura* ("Children's Literature"), No. 1 (Moscow, 1962), pages 12–103, *passim*, especially pages 15, 25, 54, and 85; and in A. Makadenov's book *Nikolai Zabolotsky* (Leningrad, 1968), pages 35–46, *passim*.

One of the rare references ever made to Kharms in print in the West is Harrison E. Salisbury's in *The 900 Days: The Siege of Leningrad* (New York, 1969), pages 170–171. Salisbury was told about Kharms by his friends in Leningrad, and calls him "a brilliant satirist, a philosopher of Gothic tendencies, a true poet of the absurd."

Sources of the Texts

All the works were translated by me from Russian typescripts, except the following: "A Play," "From a Notebook," "Symphony No. 2," "A Fable," and "The Connection" were translated from the versions in *Literaturnaya gazeta;* "Vindication," from the Czech version by Václav Daněk in *Světová literatura,* No. 6 (1968), pages 168–169, as I have not been able to obtain the Russian text; and both stories for children, from the volume *Chto eto bylo?*

Russia's Lost Literature
of the Absurd

Designed by R. E. Rosenbaum
Composed by Vail-Ballou Press, Inc.
in 10 point linotype Caledonia, 3 points leaded,
with display lines in Palatino.
Printed letterpress from type by Vail-Ballou Press
on Warren's Olde Style India, 60 pound basis,
with the Cornell University Press watermark.
Bound by Vail-Ballou Press
in Interlaken ALP book cloth
and stamped in genuine gold.
Endpapers are Strathmore Grandee Valencia Red.